"Saturated in rare immersive allure, this mesmerizing, transformational poetic delivers tremendous visceral impact. '*Āina Hānau* brilliantly entangles every aspect of kinship to birth land (water, air) integral to generations with succinct critical challenge and complete belonging embrace. Each entry deepens the experience in the pathway to an essential case laid out for justice for the peoples of the place, with matriarchal coragem guiding the way. The aunties definitely prophesied this songway. A prizewinner all the way, taking no prisoners, suffering no fools, this book makes manifest ground zero resplendent truth. What an awakening!"—**Allison Adelle Hedge Coke**, author of *Look at This Blue*

"In the tradition of poets singing, since the earliest of times, to assemble their communities in the most stirring public manner, Brandy Nālani McDougall beautifully calls forth the gathering of a people, encouraging their embrace and relearning of Kanaka ʻŌiwi culture, doing the work, in its sophisticated yet hectoring strophes, of necessary transmission and glorious praise. Yet, in the manner of late twentieth-century African, Arabic, and Caribbean poets of global consciousness, her work includes the incisive critique of political and economic hegemony, the ongoing American geographic and cultural occupation of Hawaiʻi, while at the same time providing social and personal pathways for individual decolonizations of mind. She writes as a mother, a granddaughter, a poet of politics, and a poet of elegy, ignoring no responsibility, fully aware of the range of her familial, social, and political identities. There is grandeur here, great hope, a true voice of aloha ʻāina gifted with plaintive lyricism in lament and, in critique, an heroic righteousness."—**Garrett Hongo**, author of *Coral Road*

"Brandy Nālani McDougall's second collection of poetry '*Āina Hānau / Birth Land* is a poetry that sings healing down to the realms of the occupied and to the people enduring the ruinous 'gifts of Western civilization.' Through intimate address to the poet's own people and to her daughters, we behold a retelling of a creation story where birth is synonymous with ʻāina, where responsibility to land and community winds form and stanza into a 'rope of resistance.' Watching McDougall's intimate act of reclamation and proud assertion of a sovereign heart, I am left in wakeful wonder of the connections of spirit to place, and of the poet's kuleana to a practice of radical freedom that more than resists colonization—it dismantles it line by aloha ʻāina line."—**Rajiv Mohabir**, author of *Antiman: A Hybrid Memoir*

"*ʻĀina Hānau / Birth Land* is a collection of poems that could only be written by an Indigenous Hawaiian mother; they fight to create space for Indigenous life. These are poems that speak to and for a community that contests the colonization of everything Hawaiian today—from language to bodies to homelands." —**Dan Taulapapa McMullin**, author of *Coconut Milk*

"There is a great and meticulous care with which the poet immerses herself and her reader in the love language of her people, the heart language that speaks its own truth in its inimitable ability to represent the histories, present desires, and future hope for a resilient nation."—**Lehua M. Taitano**, author of *Inside Me an Island*

'ĀINA HĀNAU
BIRTH LAND

'ĀINA HĀNAU
BIRTH LAND

BRANDY NĀLANI MCDOUGALL

ʻĀINA HĀNAU

BIRTH LAND

THE UNIVERSITY OF
ARIZONA PRESS

TUCSON

The University of Arizona Press
www.uapress.arizona.edu

We respectfully acknowledge the University of Arizona is on the land and territories of Indigenous peoples. Today, Arizona is home to twenty-two federally recognized tribes, with Tucson being home to the Oʻodham and the Yaqui. Committed to diversity and inclusion, the University strives to build sustainable relationships with sovereign Native Nations and Indigenous communities through education offerings, partnerships, and community service.

ISBN-13: 978-0-8165-4835-4 (paperback)
ISBN-13: 978-0-8165-4836-1 (ebook)

Cover design by Leigh McDonald
Cover art by Joy Lehuanani Enomoto
Interior art by Allison Leialoha Milham
Designed and typeset by Leigh McDonald in Adobe Caslon 10/14 and Worker (display)

Publication of this book is made possible in part by the proceeds of a permanent endowment created with the assistance of a Challenge Grant from the National Endowment for the Humanities, a federal agency.

Library of Congress Cataloging-in-Publication Data
Names: McDougall, Brandy Nālani, author.
Title: ʻĀina hānau = Birth land / Brandy Nālani McDougall.
Other titles: Birth land | Sun tracks ; v. 92.
Description: Tucson : University of Arizona Press, 2023. | Series: Sun tracks: an American Indian literary series; volume 92
Identifiers: LCCN 2022030132 (print) | LCCN 2022030133 (ebook) | ISBN 9780816548354 (paperback) | ISBN 9780816548361 (ebook)
Subjects: LCSH: Hawaiians—Poetry. | Hawaii—Poetry. | LCGFT: Poetry.
Classification: LCC PS3613.C394 A75 2023 (print) | LCC PS3613.C394 (ebook) | DDC 811/.6—dc23/eng/20220916
LC record available at https://lccn.loc.gov/2022030132
LC ebook record available at https://lccn.loc.gov/2022030133

Printed in the United States of America
♾ This paper meets the requirements of ANSI/NISO Z39.48-1992 (Permanence of Paper).

No nā pūnāwai oʻu e hū ai,

no Kaikainaliʻi me Kuʻuleihiwahiwa,

kuʻu mau kahawai,

no nā mamo,

no kō kākou pae ʻāina o Hawaiʻi.

Hū mai ke aloha no kuʻu ʻāina hānau.

He Mele na ke Kanaka Aloha Aina Olalo.

AOLE LOA IA E NALOWALE.

Paa kuu manao aloha,
Paa mau a paa mau,
Paa kuu manao aloha,
I ka aina hanau o'u.
Aole au e kipi,
No no no—no—no no,
Aole kumakaia,
He aloha oia mau.

Hui—Kuu lima pu me kuu
naau,
E lilo nona a nona mau,
Kuu lima pu me kuu
naau,
E lilo nona a nona mau
Paa kuu manao aloha,
Paa mau a paa mau,
Paa kuu manao aloha,
I ka aina hanau o'u.
Aloha i kuu aina,
Aloha mau aloha mau,
Mai Kaula a Niihau,
Na aina hanau o'u.
Na mauna kukilakila,
Aloha mau aloha mau,
Na kualono uli,
Ke aloha oia mau.

ALOHA AINA.

CONTENTS

'EKOLU

'EHĀ

ILLUSTRATIONS

All illustrations by Allison Leialoha Milham

‘ekahi

Ke ēwe hānau
o ka ‘āina

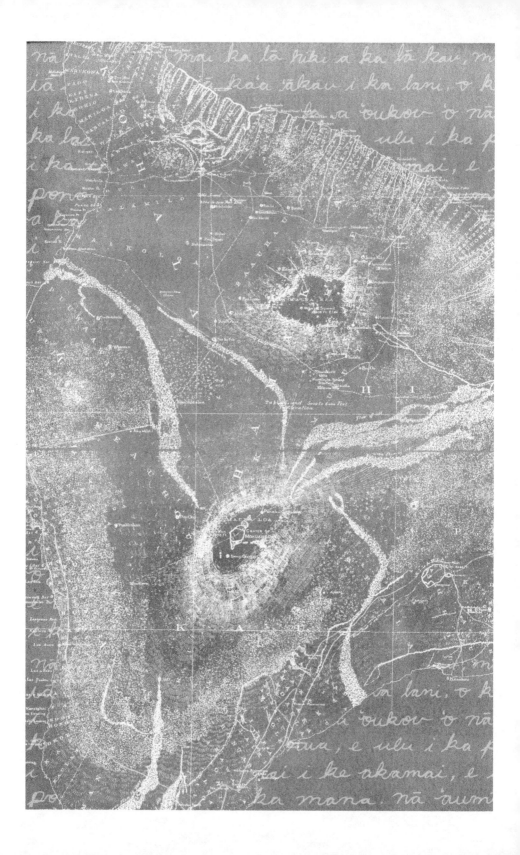

HOʻI HOU I KA IWI KUAMOʻO

I bring you coral,
bleached empty of color,
a calcified kukui husk,
palm-size red
and purple pōhaku
rounded by
the broken bones
of fish and reef,
the coarse sand, still
resembling shells

to remind you
we have always been
part ocean, part land,
that the moon
will teach us again
the right words
just beneath the water,
to know each kind
by shape and color
from the pali's vantage—

to call out for the others
to net, to return.

'ĀINA MAUNA

1.

Aloha nō
e Poliʻahu, Līlīnoe, Waiau,
Kahoupokane, Moʻoinanea, Moʻo o Kīpahulu,
Māui, Māmane, ʻAhinahina, Kalamoho, Olaliʻi, ʻIwaʻiwa,
Piliuka, ʻĀheahea, Pūkiawe, Māʻohiʻohi, Nohoanu, ʻŌhelopapa,
ʻEnaʻena, Naio, ʻAkuʻaku, Pāmakani, ʻŌhelo, Lama, ʻŌhiʻa, ʻAnunu,
Pāwale, Naʻenaʻe, ʻAʻaliʻi, Hāha, Kūkaenēnē, ʻAmaʻu, Palila, ʻAmakihi, ʻApapane,
ʻAlauahio, Tiwi, ʻElepaio, ʻAkiapolaʻau, ʻUaʻu, ʻŌpeʻapeʻa, Kiwikiu, Nēnē, me Pueo

2.

These
islands are
and will always be
the nuʻu of submerged
mauna rising from,
and rooted in,
moana, in
lipo

3.

Because our mauna are piko
between honua and lani,
between wai and kai,
between pō and ao
Because our mauna are
kumu of air and water, of thick
forests crowned with winds and mist
Because our mauna are akua unraveling all storms

4.

Mauna:
a mountain; the inland part
of an island, where land rises on all sides from the sea
to the center; a mountainous region; the name of the hard stone
from which koʻi are made; also large, swelling, extensive,
nui; māhuahua: to grow strong, to accrue; prominent;
not to be mistaken with Māuna, as in Mai Māuna:
Don't waste or dispose of uselessly

5.

When you stand with Mauna Kea and Haleakalā,
your breath becomes a warm mist carried by
cold winds. The mauna teach you to rise,
how to become ao hiwahiwa. You
hover, swallow ice seeds until
full, descend with thunder,
lightning, rain—falling
and rising again

6.

At the base camp,
we went to noon and
evening ʻaha by the kūpuna
tent and, in between, to classes
at Puʻuhuluhulu, where our kama
drew pictures of aloha ʻāina in the keiki tent,
then ate and napped on blankets, their hands cradling
pōhaku born from the mauna, the pōhaku guarding their dreams

7.

True that the whole world depends on Native bodies eating stones, linking
arms to entangle our roots, to face their guns, hoses, tear gas, tasers,

batons, dogs, and prisons, to stop their bombs, bulldozers, saws,
earth diggers, drills, cranes, toxic dumps and spills—
a thin line of Native bodies is often all
there is, and yet, we are
as immovable as
mauna

8.

2019: there
have now been five
generations of Kānaka ʻŌiwi
protecting the malu of ʻāina mauna.
They saw thousands of us aloha ʻāina, kapu
aloha, shout, "Kū kiaʻi mauna! Kū kiaʻi mauna!"
But there were thousands and thousands more behind us
they couldn't see, and there are thousands and thousands more to come

HALEAKALĀ ON GOOGLE MAPS
(SATELLITE VIEW)

You need a reservation now.
Go online and schedule
this trip several days
in advance.

Head south on Haleakalā
Highway (Route 377)
and turn before
it becomes Kekaulike
(Route 378).

You will need warm
clothes and a blanket,
a working heater
in your car.

There are 31 turns over
the 10 miles up
to the summit entrance.
Follow the long line
of cars ahead.

Answer the haole
ranger with NPS
when they ask
for confirmation
of your
reservation.

Tell them you are
Kanaka ʻŌiwi
and are here
for spiritual reasons.
You will need to answer
when you are asked
what kind of cultural
protocol you will be
following.

You will need to pay
the NPS fee anyway
because they could
not recognize you.

Quietly seethe
past Puʻunianiau.
Look down toward
the lights descending
from mountain to ocean,
the coil of cars snaking
behind you. Feel yourself
climb higher and higher
over cinders, silversword,
and tufts of sharp grass.

10 more turns
before reaching
the observatory
at the summit.
There are telescopes
here too, a new one
being built, astronomers
who only look up,
beyond even the sun,
and don't need
or have reservations.

Remember Maui
crouching in the dark,
waiting for the sun.
Remember Pele
hoping to find a home,
digging into the earth
for lava, waiting for
her sister. Remember
the aloha ʻāina
lying down to block
the trucks, arms linked
in PVC, looking up
at the stars as the
police saws started
cutting through.

Park your car and walk
across the lot. Pass
tour buses and rental
cars and find some space
within the crowd along
the railing at the edge.

Wait for your voice
to rise with the light.

THE MAP

for Clifford Nāhinu Kekauoha, Aʻapueo, Haleakalā, and Hanalei

This was always the map

from Pō   to Pō

                             You begin here

                             E haʻalele mau i ka lipolipo

          The old roads must be   there
          moonlit enough to walk

Here is when I think your favorite mele is   "Hanalei Moon"
since you played it on the organ most nights before bed.

          I played with dolls on the floor   as you handwrote
          the notes onto the manuscript paper above me

when you sang the words to find the right chords.   Here
was where you grew up, where you said every ʻohana had their own

          loʻi kalo, a māla. Here is where you made   me
          butterfish and poi, the eggs with salted water and poi

when I was sick, where you taught me to twirl   the poi
on my spoon and kahi the bowl. Here was when we laughed

          and listened to the ʻōlelo Hawaiʻi tape, asking
          each other, *No hea mai ʻoe?*   *Mahea kou ʻāina hānau?*

When you heard I was going to Hanalei, you drew me
a map of what you remembered as a child before   you left

with your ʻohana. Here is when you ask if I could find
your brother's grave. I found him with   your map

by the church where the tī grew thick and wild, and the ʻieʻie
climbed up the trunks of so many trees and   the forest felt

like it would reclaim him. Here is when you tried to send
me poi in Aotearoa twice. Where you planted   kalo,

avocado, orange, jabong, maiʻa, hung the clothes.   Here
is when you were maybe 4, the youngest keiki of 5, when you were

made to speak English only, though your mother's first
language was Cantonese and your father's was   ʻōlelo.

Here is where you joke that everyone needs to be careful
what they say around me because it could turn into   a poem.

Here is when I was 4 and you told the haole girl
next door to apologize to me for throwing   water

in my face. You were watering the plants and asked her:
What's the matter with you? How would you like it   if I did that

to you? Here is where you teach me about   germinating
seeds, algebra, how to give and take a joke, how blue light

is carried and scatters. Where we read books of moʻolelo together.
Where I can't help but think so much about you   is a poem,

where you tried to grow beans, squash, grew protea to sell
wholesale and sprayed pesticides again   and again

to save them. When you told me I couldn't have an allowance
like the haole girl next door because I get fed, clothed,   sheltered,

and loved and in return I should learn to see what needs
to be done for our ʻohana and do it.   Here is when

you asked me to help you get up, where you   watched
from bed as Hanalei flooded, the church steeple and roof

          of your old school resting just above the ʻalae   water
          as the lepo bled into the bay. That summer was wela. I got

that portable air conditioner because the fans just blew
hot air around you. Here is the first time I had to   help you

          in the bathroom, where I made the bad joke that
          I'm relieved that you're relieved   and you

groan-laughed as I told you   you're the only one
who would ever get that, as bad a joke as it is.   Here is

          when you fell,   when
          the carpet became too slippery for you to walk on,

where you mixed the poi and   kept the bowl full,
when you descaled and fried ʻakule, scraped the outer skin

          of cooked kalo and sliced the ʻiʻo,   the last
          turkey you roasted on the Weber, last 5-meat stuffing,

last pot of jook. Here was when you stopped
playing the organ at night.   I called

          the hospice nurse because   you were
          sleeping too long. You woke up, joked with her,

and later, when I walked her to her car, she told me
it's good for you to sleep,   that I have to help

          make you comfortable. I have to face you don't
          have much   time. Here

is when you asked to call the folks from church,　　　where
you sang "Hanalei Moon" with them before

　　　their blessing.　　　Here is where
　　　I became strong enough to hold you, to turn you,

to carry you, and when you stopped asking me
to help you get up.　　　Here, you asked

　　　if I was happy.　Here, you asked　　　if I
　　　was *sure* that I was happy.

　　　　　It was Pō'akahi when the last hua 'ōlelo
　　　　　you learned was lawa. Just a little poi. No more
　　　　　medicine. Lawa already.　　　You said.

　　　　　Pō'alua, when I started sleeping in the chair
　　　　　next to your bed because there was a ghost
　　　　　you kept seeing　　　in the corner.

　　　　　Pō'akolu, when you slept most of the day,
　　　　　where I realized too late that there were too
　　　　　many lasts in the past few years　　　and days.

　　　　　Pō'ahā when you seemed like yourself again
　　　　　and asked me to wheel you outside on the deck
　　　　　to see the sky and　　　Haleakalā in the ahiahi
　　　　　as the moon was rising. Finally a cool breeze
　　　　　as you looked over that darkening 'āina of fruit
　　　　　trees and flowered green you planted, orange-pink
　　　　　streaks piercing the clouds as the sun sank.　　　Ua lawa.

　　　　　Pō'alima when you kept sleeping, started
　　　　　gasping like　　　'a'ohe lawa.

　　　　　Pō'aono when—you stopped it all—when all of us
　　　　　were out of the room,　　　when all of us
　　　　　thought there'd be more time,　　　when

'a'ohe lawa ka manawa

we thought we'd be with you,   when

you end and begin   end and begin.

Lawa pono 'ole kēia mau hua 'ōlelo
e hanohano i kou 'āina hānau,
e hanohano i ka 'āina hānau
āu i ho'okumu ai no ka 'ohana

This was always the map

from Pō   to Pō

The roads are said to edge

toward
a lele overlooking the ocean

You would have walked down
the mountain from A'apueo.

E ho'i mau i ka uliuli

I'll look for you

here

where

when

there

THE KAHULUI MCDONALD'S

It was the Kahului McDonald's—
all the way down the mountain
in town, each morning wiped
of saliva, boogers, spilled or barfed
milkshakes, and left shining color,
fiberglass cool, new again, and
waiting, green turfgrass swept
to erase the day before—

that had the best playground,
the one for big-but-not-too-big kids,
saddled fry guys on springs that you
could ride and bend to nearly touch
the ground, a Hamburglar tunnel
only we could fit in, where grown-ups
couldn't see. Remember?

We crawled up into the mouth
of Officer Big Mac whose teeth
were silver bars to pretend
we were in jail, sat, unstrapped,
on a purple Grimace carousel,
whirling and hanging, showing off
by holding on with just our legs,
our heads thrown backward,
hair combing the plastic grass.

We wished then that McDonald's
might come home with us back up
the mountain, but in the end
it was always too shiny and clean
for us, its new gleam too dizzying.

KŪKAʻŌʻŌ HEIAU ON GOOGLE MAPS (SATELLITE VIEW)

University meets Dole
at Bachman Lawn

Metcalf runs parallel
to Dole and intersects
University just one block
mauka across Sinclair

Up farther,
Vancouver
connects University
to McKinley,
which you can take
to Beckwith

If you go up
even farther,
University
becomes
Oʻahu

and runs past
Kūkaʻōʻō Heiau
(Mānoa Heritage Center),
which can only
be accessed
via one
of the Cooke houses,
which they named
Kūaliʻi. Tours

run for $7 by
appointment only

Heading mauka
from O'ahu, take
a left on Cooper
to get to Mānoa
to get to Kūali'i
to get to Kūka'ō'ō

It's there—
in the piko
of foreign trees
and multimillion-
dollar homes
owned, or
once owned,
by missionaries,
on land that
will always
belong to
Lono

You pass it every day
without knowing

REAL (G)ESTATE

I.

as in not
imagined,
fraudulent
or illusory

as in property
consisting of land
and/or buildings

as in assets,
an extensive area
of land and money
owned by a person,
especially at death

as in possession
of land by virtue
of a legal document

as in   by law
        by paper
        by lethal force
        if necessary
        (and it's always
        necessary)

as in carrying
a life
in your womb
as in feeding
that life
from your
body

as in feeding
a life from
'āina after
she/he/they
have left
your body

as in deeds
are written
to record and prove
the ownership
of   'āina

as in deeds have
been stolen, changed,
or lost without kūpuna
knowing or because
they couldn't pay

as in who will
be, are and have
been squatters,
occupants

as in who will
be, are and have
been owners,
discoverers

as in what
is real?

as in at the time
of this writing
Hawaiʻi is the
most expensive
fake state in the
United States

as in the median
price of homes in
2021 was $1.06 million
up 22% from 2020
and is much higher
as you read this

as in home equity
appreciation on stolen
Indigenous land is
the greatest single
source of American
wealth, accounting

the taxes or for food
or because they were
too trusting and no
matter which were too
shame to fight or didn't
think they could

as in ʻŌiwi can be heirs to
ʻāina   we didn't know
we had until we see letters
declaring adverse possession
from Carlsmith Ball LLP
on behalf of developers

as in U.S.
property law
legalizes
historical and
ongoing theft

as in U.S.
systemic racism
and colonialism
determine property
values and who
can qualify for
mortgage loans

as in how we must buy
ʻāina   we can't afford
ʻāina   we must protect
ʻāina   e ola, e kanu
ʻāina   so those who lived

for 34% of U.S.
household net worth

'āina   in our wombs will know
'āina   here is
          'ohana

2.

as in Hawai'i's
numbah 1 and 2
economic industreez—
tourism and da U.S.
military—increase
inflation, housing
prices, and da overall
cost of living

as in aia i hea
da real cost-
benefit analysis?
cuz da only ting
dey tell us is
everyting maika'i

as in vacation rentos
earn mo' $ den regulah
rentos, so make sense
dat da few long-term
rentos dat stay, dey inflated

as in almos' 25%
of homes ova hea
are bought by
out-of-fake-state
peepos and plenny

as in 'iewe are sacred,
must be
treated as sacred,
must be
planted in sacred
'āina

as in 'o Honolulu
ka 'āina hānau
o ku'u mau kamali'i
and their 'iewe have been
in my freezer since
they were born, moved
from freezer to freezer
from rental to rental

as in they are now
9 and 5 years old
and I have to move
their 'iewe sometimes
as I search for meat
to defrost for dinner
or for the popsicles
my oldest daughter loves

stay tourists buying
vacation homes
dey going visit
only once a yea

as in tousands
in da military who
no live on-base use
housing allowances
dey get to rent
off-base and cuz
da allowances stay
above fair market
rents, dey can edge
out local rentas and
drive up rento prices

as in da military
does live-fire
training—burning
bombing shooting—
on land dat could
grow food or have
real affordable
housing

as in sumbody
please let deez
politicians know
dat affordable
housing not
affordable if we
cannot qualify

as in I am a single mom
raising two girls, renting
a 2-bedroom apartment
in Honolulu and despite
being a tenured professor
at UH, half my paycheck
goes to rent alone

as in the other half
of my paycheck
goes to food, gas,
utilities, medical,
dental, insurance,
and preschool tuition

as in I see their
ʻiewe every day
behind the popsicles
and meat and must
resist thinking
of their ʻiewe laʻa
as popsicles or meat

as in on most days I feel farther
from ʻāina   than ever
before and think please don't
let my daughters see
their own children's ʻiewe
in their freezers, please
let them know the malu of
ʻāina   the kuleana of
ʻāina   please please please

as in Hawai'i is
da second most
expensive fake
state fo' rentas

as in aia i hea
da back rent—
and not jus' §5(f)—
owed to us 'Ōiwi?

3.

as in 46,255 'Ōiwi
applicants who meet
the high 50% blood
quantum criteria in
the Hawaiian Homes
Commission Act
are waiting on the list
(most for decades)

as in if you are awarded
a residential lot, you pay
a dollar to lease the land,
but need to also afford
a 10% down payment
and qualify for a
mortgage of $300,000
to build a house
or to purchase one
from a developer

as in if you die,
your spouse and

as in at least I have
a freezer and can
(for now) afford
meat and popsicles

as in ku'u ēwe,
ku'u piko, ku'u
iwi, ku'u koko

as in my daughters
are the beautiful
mo'o of all their kūpuna—
Kanaka 'Ōiwi, CHamoru,
Chinese, Scottish (and
more), and NOT
mathematical equations
in the racist fraud that is
American blood logic

as in I was 36 and hāpai
with my first keiki
in a birth class for 'Ōiwi
'ohana when I learned
our kūpuna planted
our 'iewe in
'āina   so
'āina   would
always be a part of us

as in neither my 'Ōiwi
mother and father nor

children must prove
they have at least 25%
blood quantum to inherit
the house you own
on the lot you lease
or they will lose the land
and the house (since the
land is what matters and
none of you ever really
owned the land)

as in their children
and their children and
their children and so on
will need to maintain
the minimum 25%
blood quantum to remain
in the house on the land
and like you, will need
to choose who to have
children with accordingly

as in Hawaiian
Home Land "lessees"
pay property taxes
based on fee simple
property valuations
but are not allowed
to access or benefit
from their equity

as in at the rate
DHHL has developed
residential lots over

my ʻŌiwi grandparents
learned the importance
of planting ʻiewe and
I don't know how far
back we go without
ʻiewe kanu

as in conflicts over
land   have
led to oki   in our
ʻohana   uncles
aunties   cousins
sisters   brothers
we stopped   knowing

as in who was left what
and who should have
been left what and who
was promised what and
who has what now

as in who can afford
to keep   ʻāina
or who is least likely
to lose   ʻāina
through divorce or debt

and there was never
enough   ʻāina
for everyone

we were all
sheltered once, fed

the past 30 years,
it would take 182
years to meet the
demand for those
on the waitlist now

as in 95% of applicants
on the waitlist will die
waiting for land

as in at the time
of this writing
the fake state settled
a lawsuit for $328 million
for mismanagement
of the public lands
trust, but the amount
of damages each
beneficiary is owed
still needs to be
determined (though
it will not be enough)

as in aren't we all
on a waitlist?

from our mothers'
ʻāina

as in those of us
who have been able
to keep ʻiewe know
we need
ʻāina   to kanu
and without
ʻāina   we keep
their ʻiewe
in our freezers
or our sheltered
family's freezers
hoping we have
ʻāina   someday

as in for those
of us who don't have
ʻiewe kanu, are we
doomed to always feel
buried (not planted)?

as in nā ēwe
o ka ʻāina

4.

as in Kānaka ʻŌiwi
have the highest
poverty rates of
the 5 largest race
groups in the fake state

as in the per capita

as in the U.S. is built
on the lie of white property
rights over Native lands and
BIPOC, womyn, queer, and
disabled bodies, labor, and
creative and intellectual
cultures, and yet there is no

income for ʻŌiwi
was $20,664
(or 31% below
the fake state
average) in 2018

as in nearly 50%
of sheltered ʻŌiwi
households experience
problems of affordability,
overcrowding, or
structural inadequacy

as in over 50%
of all unsheltered
people in Hawaiʻi
identify as
Native Hawaiian
or Pacific Islander

as in Hawaiʻi's
unsheltered people
are criminalized
and incarcerated
for sitting or lying
down on sidewalks
(or even just walking
around peacefully)
in many Hawaiʻi
neighborhoods

as in unsheltered
people have been
found to live 30

safety for ʻiewe   from
being dug up,   removed,
destroyed   without
being part   of that lie

as in only now can I admit
that I have stayed in abusive
relationships for financial
security and the promise
of homeownership

as in I have a history
of building homes
with dysfunction
and denial

as in doesn't
everyone in Hawaiʻi?
everyone in the lands
now known as
the United States?

as in what would
my life have been
like if my ʻiewe
had been planted?

as in our ʻiewe
house the mana
of mother and child

as in ʻiewe
are planted in ceremony

years less than
sheltered people here

as in unsheltered
people in Hawai'i
are made out to be
criminals, druggies,
and crazies that need
to be hidden or locked
away (since we're all
supposed to be happy
colonized natives here)
when they are both
the survivors and
the evidence of
real violent crimes

as in we need
an unsheltered
ceremony to
redline the violent lie
of this American dream

as in
mai poina:
we were all
sheltered once

to tie the child
to that   'āina,
to give them
their kuleana
to that   'āina,
to guide them
always
toward that   'āina,

as in how else did/do/will
our keiki know
'āina   hānau?
'āina   aloha?
'āina   mo'o?
'āina   who we are?

as in my dream
is for
my kamali'i
to know
belonging
without
longing

we were all sheltered
once, fed from our
mother 'āina

KA HANA MAU LOA

There is always the work
of mending and clearing

to be done, the long
entwined branches, newly

trimmed off an old tree
hauled to the bordering gulch,

and the sweet smell of smoke
carried by the wind. Above,

the clouds fracture
into unmapped pathways,

bend, slowly, to seed
themselves back

       down into the soil.

'elua

*Kalo kanu
o ka 'āina*

"Kou aina hanau—e,
Nou au e mele nei."

O ka Poalua,
M. H. ...
me ka ...

... wale ke aloha i ka aina,
A' nei puuwai e hiipoi nei.
Me he la a e i mai ana,
Ne hopo iho na Hawaii,
... aloha i ka aina,
... e ka lenakili
... e hopo ana.
... Kahiki,
... i hai ...
... ui,
... a...
... in

... na aina,
... nui nei,
... Kalaun...
... hoa,
... lahui,
... na o ka
... hee;
... hoa na kaula
... na kau i ka
... a nona mau,
... pu me kuu
... aina a nona ma...
... uua mana i aloha
... au a pa...au,
... kuu

Na kualono uli,
Ke aloha oia mau.

Olao,
A E SILOWALE,
Ke aloha oia mau,
Paa kou manao aloha,
ALOHA AINA.

POI-KU

Light stirred into earth.
Wai stirred into pa'i'ai.
Huli replanted.

The mākua share.
The keiki have their own bowls.
No fish in the poi.

Nothing in the poi
but poi, and kahi the sides
of the bowl when pau.

Ke'ala's forehead
after Christmas dinner: How
did poi get up there?

Early memory: poi
dries around your mouth like skin,
like it always was.

THE KING KAMEHAMEHA STATUE ON GOOGLE MAPS (MAP VIEW)

The King Kamehameha statue
looks smaller than you think.

To his left,
Mililani Street
runs two ways.
To his right,
Punchbowl
moves only makai.

He stands,
his back to Aliʻiolani
and Queen.
He faces South King Street
heading to Diamond Head,
his arm still
extending toward
a beige box
in an open
gray field
named ʻIolani Palace.

It is just beyond reach.

CHARACTER DEVELOPMENT

in the Kamehameha classroom, grade 9

It must be hard to hold
so much back when you hear
the wind whiffling through
the near-empty halls of Pākī,
reminding you of where you
just walked so freely between
periods. When I remind you
that class has begun, you pull
the book out of your backpack,
wanting mostly to check
your social media, and happy
that a pretty girl or boy smiled
and just talked to you; you are
red faced after running uphill,
and tired after your parents
fought all night about money. Or worse.

I know enough, having lived
longer, that some of you will
become the doctors and lawyers
your parents want or are afraid
to want, that you will teach
hula and comparative literatures,
raise children who speak Hawaiian,
you will leave your ʻāina,
by choice or force, write mele
and testimony. You will know
or never know where or how
America lies, how to steal
for more drugs, or how it feels
to cross a street without

caring if a car hits you. Either way
you will try to heal, remembering
the wind in the halls, though some
of your families will lose you
in all the ways a person gets lost.

But this is only the character,
who can be static or dynamic,
acting, interacting, and reacting,
carving pathways through
conflict in a predetermined
series of options. This is you
being acted upon, and perhaps,
this is as it should be or
as it was always meant to be,
though I know this is little comfort.

I ask you to open your books
because, in the meantime,
there are important things
you need to know about
longing and belonging,
the space between spoken
and truth. There are quotes
you need to learn to cite
and commas you must place
in the empty spaces where
you must breathe or break
phrases apart without
the finality of the period.

I don't tell you why
these are important things
you need to know, and the
school setting is such that
you don't even bother to ask.

But if it was in my character
to be more courageous,
I would tell you honestly
that a part of me must believe
words can save us if we open
ourselves fully, if we can name
the ones who spoke before us,
and we, unbroken, still
have the breath to speak them.

SYMBOLISM

in the Kamehameha classroom, grade 9

You want to know why
something can't just be itself—
why kalo is family,
a wa'a is hope,
a shark is danger,
even as it is ancestor,
and the rye field
is innocence.

Because there is always
a deeper meaning,
I tell you, and find
answers among the pages
for all of your *whys*:

weaving is never just
weaving, and moths, gardens
and houses and stray dogs,
flashlights, red hats, and
shoes must always be more
than they seem. They are
tradition, cultural shame,
justice, individualism, hope,
fate, and colonialism, and not
necessarily in that order.
They are love and death
and rebirth and God.

I'm teaching you to see
like me, and I can't see
a cloud or a river or

a stone without its history
or consequence,
a glimpse of its conclusion.

Like a paranoid tyrant,
I declare that everything is
everything *else* and demand
you take notes because I can't
remember a time I didn't think
to look for what was hidden,
(as inevitably, all things are)
to read the signs and be
ready for the thing that has
never just been itself.

I am beginning to suspect
you already know what I
still need to learn: to trust
things to be without bending
their shape, to let go, finally,
of what only seems like more.

COLONIALISM

in the Kamehameha classroom, grade 9

You want to know if this means
that colonialism is everything

we now know and do—
our clothes? our food? our music? our God?

I don't have the answers
you want. In your short life so far

you want to wear, eat, and listen
to what you see on TV

and God speaks to you through
Beyoncé and the kahu's guitar

on chapel Thursdays and on Sundays
if you are a boarder. You don't want

to be different. You want the freedom
and joy that is promised you

in McDonald's spam and egg breakfasts,
in Jamba smoothies.

Jesus tells you this is how it should be
if you want to be good,

that the old Gods of our kūpuna,
that the ancestors of our ancestors

are only stories you shouldn't believe.
But when you walk the land

surf the ocean, when you feel
the slough and ooze of mud

and sand between your toes
you know we are caught between

our 'āina and their distant holy land,
our moana and their Deluge.

Kū and Hina feed our people
Kāne and Kanaloa feed our people

Maui brings the fire
Pele brings the fire

Lono greens the earth
Hi'iaka greens the earth

but Jesus takes the credit.
My own answers are too bitter,

too hopeless for you, I know—
colonialism is everything around you

but it is not you, it doesn't need to be.

The pueo and manō circle
above you and beneath you

to lead you back, then forward.

COLLEGE PREP TEST FOR THOSE WHO WILL LEAVE HAWAI'I

in the Kamehameha classroom, grade 11

Match the following questions (on the left) with their answers on the right.

1) "Hawaiian" just means you're from Hawai'i, right?

A) Are you a *real*, I mean *pure*, haole?

2) Are you a *real*, I mean *pure*, Hawaiian?

E) "American" just means you're blissfully ignorant of profiting off of stolen people and stolen lands, right?

3) How did you learn to speak English so good?

I) You should educate yourself (perhaps in the grammar of your own language) before you embarrass yourself.

4) How much Hawaiian are you?

O) Define "Racism."

5) Why are you guys so racist against white people?

U) It was the United States that violated all of its treaties with Indigenous nations, and who violated international law by supposedly annexing Hawai'i without a treaty. There is no land claimed by the United States that wasn't stolen, no Indigenous nation that wasn't subjected to (ongoing) genocide.

6) Would you have rather been taken over by the Japanese?

7) Why don't you people just get over it already?

H) Last time I checked, Hawaiians weren't preventing haoles from getting jobs, stealing land from haoles, and exploiting haole culture for tourist money.

K) How much haole are you?

L) Kū i ka pono! Kū kia'i mauna! Kū'ē!

M) Kūpa'a ma hope o ka 'āina.

N) He mamo a Hāloa au.

P) Ua lawa mākou i ka pōhaku.

W) He Hawai'i au mau a mau.

STAR-SPANGLED BANNER

A betrayal
to stand
with your hand
over your heart
and sing
the song

of the country
occupying
your country

to read every star
on the flag
above
your country's flag

and see the last one
there: small, white,
and pointed

stitched into the blue
with a thin thread

as if
it has always
been that way

as if
it can never
be undone.

AMERICAN POEM

This is my American poem
starving and helpless in an unknown land,
searching for religious freedom,
vulnerable to the kindnesses
of violent savages.

This is my American poem
calculating how to fill the ship
with chained Africans, lying
horizontal and stacked to the ceiling
of the lower decks, while
minimizing human wastage.

This is my American poem
built on the bones of Natives
and African slaves, of indentured
or otherwise exploited Asian,
Latinx, and Pacific Islander
laborers, saving some for
museum exhibits.

This is my American poem
speaking of freedom and freely
speaking, yet rarely saying anything
to set land and people free.

This is my American poem
sucking the earth's metals,
minerals, and oil through
a straw longer and older
than Keystone XL
or DAPL or Line 3.

This is my American poem
paying the police to crack
down violently on protectors
while paying politicians
to fine them for obstruction.

This is my American poem
fracking the sand, the soil
for ounces of black petroleum
and placing fuel tanks by
aquifers, contaminating
gallons of potable water.

This is my American poem
drilling for oil in the Arctic
Refuge then uploading videos
to YouTube of the last glaciers
calving (hoping it will go viral).

This is my American poem
taking refuge in an embassy,
thankful for military bases
in hostile territory, testing sites
in Indian country, in Alaska,
in the Atlantic, in the Pacific.

This is my American poem
dropping bombs on islands,
dropping guns for puppet
governments, dropping cans
of carcinogenic meats
for war-torn refugees.

This is my American poem
screaming that we should take
care of our own before helping others.

This is my American poem
holding title to a continent,
to islands, to oceans, patenting
genetic modifications to own
and profit from all that grows green.

This is my American poem,
developing and selling houses
built on toxic dump sites, piping
water poisoned to acceptable levels.

This is my American poem,
ravenous and desperate for its next
frontier, plagued with acid reflux
and irritable bowel syndrome
after all it has eaten.

This is my American poem
speaking before millions
in an expensive Italian suit,
hoping its comb-over won't
lift off its scalp unexpectedly.

This is my American poem,
tired after spending money to
save money, after brawling
over bargains on Black Friday,
which started last Thursday.

This is my American poem
using excessive violence,
shooting children in hoodies and
beating Black relatives (to death)
in custody, giving itself
reasonable cause.

This is my American poem
securing the perimeter of
the electric fence, ready to shoot
anyone the searchlight touches.

This is my American poem
separating children from
their families, putting them
in cages, only to deny them asylum.

This is my American poem
taking away the constitutional
right to abortion and forcing
all birthing bodies to bring
any pregnancy to term
no matter the mental,
physical, or financial costs.

This is my American poem
forgetting where it came from,
losing its songs, its stories,
its languages, clearing its
plants and animals, breaking
its promises.

This is my American poem
protecting the earth's wild places
from the wild peoples who protected
the earth for thousands
of generations before.

This is my American poem
wanting to do the right thing, but
wanting more for the right thing
to make money, to keep power.

This is my American poem
buying buying buying
stocks and hedge funds
just before the president declares war
and selling selling selling
long before the troops
get restationed elsewhere.

This is my American poem
turning to smile for the cameras,
shaking hands with lesser
but useful dignitaries.

This is my American poem
completely absent
but politely present
through UN testimony and
climate change summits.

This is my American poem
suppressing how nothing
so broken can survive
nor can anything
that has broken
so many.

This is my American poem
imagining its only end
coming postapocalyptic
solar flare, zombie epidemic,
climate change catastrophe,
or alien invasion,
but even then believing
it will live on as
the best poem ever written.

THIS ISLAND ON WHICH I LOVE YOU

And when, on this island on which
I love you, there is only so much land
to drive on, a few hours to encircle
in entirety, and the best of our lands
are touristed, the beaches foam-laced
with rainbowing suntan oil,
the mountains tattooed with asphalt,
pocked by telescoped domes,
hotels and luxury condos blighting
the line between ocean and sky,

I find you between the lines
of such hard edges, sitting on
the kamyo stool, a bowl of coconut,
freshly grated, at your feet.

That I hear the covert jackaling
of helicopters and jets overhead
all night through our open jalousies,
that my throat burns from the scorch
of the grenaded graves of my ancestors,
the vog that smears the Koʻolaus into a blur
of greens, that I wake to hear the grind
of you blending vegetables and fruit,
machine whirl-crunching coffee beans,
your shoulder blades channeling
ocean, a steady flux of current.

Past the guarded military testing grounds,
amphibious assault vehicles emerging
from the waves, beyond the tangles
of tarp cities lining the roads, past
the thick memory of molasses coating

the most intimate coral crevices,
by the box jellyfish congregating under
'Ole Pau and Kāloa moons, at the park
beneath the emptied trees, I come
to find you shaking five-dollar coconuts
(because this is all we have on this island),
listening to the water to guess
its sweetness and youth.

On this island on which I love you,
something of you is in the rain rippling
through the wind that makes the pipes
of Waikīkī burst open, long brown
fingers of sewage stretch out
from the canal, and pesticided
tendrils flow from every ridge
out to sea, and so we stay inside
to bicker over how a plumeria tree
moves in the wind, let our daughters
ink lines like coarse rootlets
in our notebooks, crayon lines
into ladders on our walls
and sheets. Their first sentences
are sung, moonlit blowhole plumes
of sound that call pebbles to couple,
caverns to be carved, 'uala to roll
down the hillside again, and I could
choke on this gratitude for you all.

This island is alive with love,
its storms, the cough of alchemy
expelling every parasitic thing,
teaching me to love you with
the intricacies of island knowing,
to depend on the archipelagic
spelling of you lying next to me,
to trust in the shape and curve
of your hand reaching out to hold mine.

RESIST

For Palestine, in solidarity

Qawem ya sha'abi, qawemhum. *Resist, my people, resist them.*
—DAREEN TATOUR

Hawaiians are still here. We are still creating, still resisting.
—HAUNANI-KAY TRASK

Stand in rage as wind and current clash
                              rile lightning and thunder
fire surge and boulder crash

        Let the ocean eat and scrape away these walls
Let the sand swallow their fences whole
                    Let the air between us split the atmosphere

We have no land   No country
          But we have these bodies   these stories
this language of rage   left

        This resistance is bitter
and tastes like medicine   Our lands
          replanted in the dark and warm   there

We unfurl our tangled roots   stretch
                    to blow salt across
          blurred borders of memory

          They made themselves
fences and bullets   checkpoints
          gates and guard posts   martial law

They made themselves
   hotels and mansions adverse
possession   eminent domain and deeds

   They made themselves
           shine
       through the plunder

They say we can never—They say
    we will never—because
   because they—

     and the hills and mountains have been
mined for rock walls   the reefs
   pillaged for coral floors

They say we can never—
      and the deserts and dunes have been
shoveled and taken for their houses and highways—

    because we can never—because
the forests have been raided   razed
   and scorched and we   we the wards

refugees   houseless   present-
absentees   recognition refusers   exiled
uncivilized   disposable   natives

protester-activist-terrorist-resisters—
    our springs and streams have been
dammed—so they say we can never return   to

     let it go   accept this
progress   stop living
  in the past—

but we make ourselves
        strong enough to carry all of our dead
                engrave their names in the clouds

We gather to sing whole villages awake
        We crouch down to eat rocks like fruit
                to hold the dirt   the sand
        in our hands

to fling words
        the way fat drops of rain
                splatter off tarp or corrugated roofs

We remember the sweetness   We rise from the plunder
        They say there is no return   yet

                they never could really make us leave

THE SECOND GIFT

for Haunani

The first gift of Western civilization was disease.
The second gift of Western civilization was violence.

—HAUNANI-KAY TRASK

I.

I have no mercy or compassion in me for a society that will crush people,
and then penalize them for not being able to stand up under the weight.

—MALCOLM X

For over four generations
they have said we are
a people with a history
of violence, accustomed to
the dark, cold cell, remedial
in mind and body. They write
of how we killed infants,
sacrificed humans, practiced
incest, how our kings and queens
were alcoholic, inept dictators,
how we owned slaves, how
disease comes with darkness,
how they must save us
from ourselves.

          And we take
the new tongue and its historical
revisions, the low test scores,
the longer sentences, the water
shortages, the paid-off politicians,
the third part-time jobs, the cancers

and the radiation, diabetes
and the amputations, eminent
domain and adverse possession,
the overruling of all our objections
because now
their violence
is all we know.

2.

We are not American! We are not American! We are not American!
—HAUNANI-KAY TRASK

Violence is more than lodging
bullets into Brown or Black
bodies, but also burning
sacred valleys, stabbing tunnels
into mountains, damming streams,
building telescopes on our mauna,
dumping poisons into oceans,
overdeveloping 'āina, bombing
and buying islands. Violence is
Arizona jail cells, GMOs,
and unearthed iwi waiting
under a Walmart ramp, in boxes
in museums, in a church basement.
Violence is what we settle for
because we've been led to believe
green paper can feed us
more than green land.

Violence is what we're used to
as they measure our blood
to wait decades for a dollar-a-year
lease, when we forget how we once
fed and healed ourselves, how
our mouths hold life and death.

We are no longer shocked
by raids on what is left
in the pitched tents and tarps,
our evictions from beach to beach
and park to park, the poverty
of unfurling fists open only
to the smallest of handouts.

Violence is believing
you are in the United States
driving on a highway
built over the sacred,
carrying artillery to scorch
the sacred so more sacred lands
can become the United States
through violence.

3.

Don't let anybody tell you not to be angry. We have every right to be
angry—this is our country.

—HAUNANI-KAY TRASK

You were born
into captivity,
a Native in a racist,
anti-Native world;
yet, they call *you* racist.
They hate you
like they have hated
every warrior before you.

This helps them bear
the weight of dominion;
helps them keep their vacation
houses, golf courses, hotels,
and bases; helps them feed

their children denial,
so as adults they, too,
can say, "Don't blame me
for what happened
a hundred years ago."
They must keep
believing that
the United States
is our country
and not just
the country
that occupies
our country,
Hawai'i.

4.

It always seems impossible until it's done.
—NELSON MANDELA

You tell us:
"You are not a racist
because you fight racism.
You are a warrior,"
and you train more warriors,
show us how to sharpen
and land words like spears,
how to catch their spears
and hurl them back.
You call us the spears
of our nation, assure us,
"Decolonization is all
around us." You guide us
to the rope of resistance
so we can weave
the newest strands together
under a sovereign sun.

And so we tell our children,
our children tell their children,
and their children tell their children
until our words become
the chattering winds of hope
that erode the hardness of violence
from the earth, and we are sown
back into
          and born from
              Papahānaumoku

                  green and tender once again.

'ekolu

*Hānau
ka 'āina,
hānau
ke ali'i,
hānau
ke kanaka*

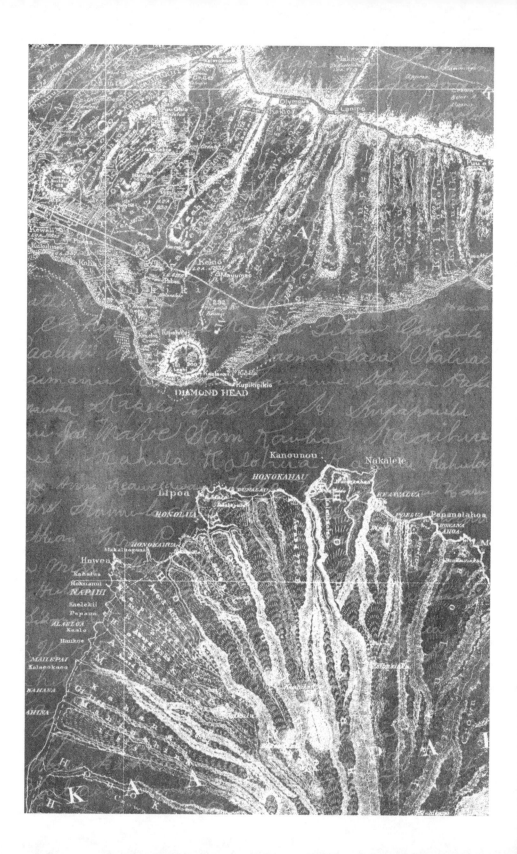

PREPOSITIONS

1.   between

    these   words

            islands live

2.   under

    a closing proximity

    separate   skies of

                            constellations rising

3.   over

                    so many words
                        yet   unsaid
    from   our
    languages
    as   they
    fill
    this space

4.   out

    of   salt
    water   behind

    reefs   of cloud cover
    that keep
    us
            symbolic where

we stand

5.   in
      this ocean

      woven by water   when
      we kiss

      the long   untold

      journey   of a blue
      jellyfish   ends

      floating

6.   through
      this last   distance

      our bodies   still
      untouched

      like whole   tentacles
      threading   themselves

7.   into

      the sand
      as endless as   salt

      water   washing   over

      the sting
         finally buried

8.   under
      us

9.   above
         us

10.   as
         the low tide exposes

         our closeness

11.   alongside.

FROM POEM FOR THE CANCEL RIMPAC COALITION

A Collaborative Poem with Poets of Aotearoa, the Federated States of Micronesia, Guåhan, and Hawaiʻi

In a world without RIMPAC,

                there is breath

        enough—to stand

against the torpedoing teeth,

      the amphibious assaults,

        underwater explosions,

           the nuclear bombs

           and billions

      of dollars and bullets

        of peacetime that continue

                  elsewhere—

          breath enough

        to salve these

      and so many wounds,

to sing so loud

    we drown

        all submarine sonar.

HONOKĀHUA ON GOOGLE MAPS (SATELLITE THEN STREET THEN SATELLITE VIEW)

Your first attempt to find
Honokāhua seems wrong.
You know it should be
in Lahaina, but you are placed
amid the cinder cones
of Haleakalā. Wonder
if Google knows
Honokāhua is an ahupuaʻa.

Your second attempt
leads to choices:
Honokāhua Bay, Maui County, HI
Honokāhua Burial Site, Lahaina, HI
Honokāhua Stream, Maui County, HI
Honokāhua Street, Honolulu, HI

The last of these is not your destination.

You satellite-view the bay,
see Honoapiʻilani Highway
(State Route 30)
first hugging the coastline
then run mauka away
from Plantation Estates Drive
and Plantation Club Drive.
See the wide roofs
of multimillion-dollar
houses, fenced and gated,

with pools and ocean views,
hugging the evenly
green golf course.

Street-view and insist on taking
Lower Honoapiʻilani Road. You
want to see what was here
before the asphalt, the manicured
hau and bougainvillea bushes.
The well-placed, coconut-less palms.
Wonder, instead, if there is just one big
golf course or several in a cluster.
See more multimillion-dollar
houses that look like all the others.

A crossed steeple rises
on your right—a church. Turn left
to park. A sign reads:
Honokāhua Burial Site
Registered as a state historic place
Deeded to the State of Hawaii
Public entry is prohibited
Please kōkua

Your street view ends, so
you zoom out. You need
to walk 0.6 miles (about 10 minutes)
past the Napili Wing
and crucifix-shaped pool
of the five-diamond hotel
honoring the beauty and traditions
of Hawaii—the Ritz-Carlton.

Look past the men
setting up the white chairs,
the plumeria walkway,
the arch swirled in chiffon to frame
the sunset ocean wedding.

Try to see what was here
before the landscaped naupaka
boundary, before there was
Honokāhua Preservation.

Try to see what was here
when the dunes were dug up,
then sliced into tiers. See
our kūpuna laid bare.

See our people holding signs:

Na Wai e Hoʻola i nā Iwi?
Stop Digging Hawaiian Bones
Kapu the Bones
Leave Our Ancestors Alone
Mai Kaulaʻi Wale i nā Iwi Kupuna

See our people stopping
bulldozers, then archaeologists.
See our people learning to make
kapa to wrap the hundreds of iwi.
See them waiting for the aumoe
to replant the bones of our kūpuna
in the maluhia of darkness.

See, in the distance, the glowing
outline of the koholā's fin slapping
the ocean's surface, the pueo circling
overhead, all the moonlit hōʻailona
showing you the way forward and back.

WATER REMEMBERS

Waikīkī was once a fertile marshland
ahupuaʻa, mountain water gushing
from the valleys of Makiki, Mānoa,
Pālolo, Waiʻalae, and Wailupe
to meet ocean water. Seeing such
wealth, kānaka planted hundreds
of fields of kalo, ʻuala, ʻulu in the uka,
built fishponds in the muliwai.
Waikīkī fed Oʻahu people for generations,
so easily that its ocean raised surfers,
hailed the highest of aliʻi to its shores.

Waikīkī is now a miasma of concrete
and asphalt, its waters drained
into a canal dividing tourist from resident.
The mountain's springs and waterfalls,
trickling where they are allowed to flow
and left stagnant elsewhere, pullulate
with staphylococcus. In the uplands,
the fields have long been dismantled,
their rock terraces and heiau looted
to build the walls of multimillion-dollar
houses with panoramic Diamond Head
and/or ocean views. Closer to the ocean,
hotels fester like pustules, the sand
stolen from other ʻāina to manufacture
the beaches, seawalls maintained
to keep the sand in so suntan-oiled
tourists can laze on what never was,
what never should have been. No one
is fed plants and fish from this ʻāina now—
its land value has grown so that nothing
but money *can* be grown—its waters unpotable, polluted.

Each year as heavy rainfalls flood the valleys,
spill over gulches, slide the foundations
of overpriced houses, invade sewage pipes
and send brown-water runoff to the ocean,
the king tides roll in, higher in their warming,
lingering longer and breaking through
sandbags and barricades, eroding the resorts.

This is not the end of civilization but
a return to one. Only the water insisting
on what it should always have, spreading
its liniment over infected wounds. Only
the water rising above us, reteaching us
wealth and remembering its name.

PU'ULOA

Outside our home:
pregnant sprawl of American war
and selective memory—protrusion
of concrete roadway, white bar
hovering over the rusted wrecks
of turrets, barnacled oil bunkers,
torpedo blisters. Lokoamano, drained,
filled to build the naval yard. Docked
battleships in service, Moku'ume'ume
enclosed, metal earth-mover claws, hooks
       ever ready to ravage awalau under
       the great white eyeball of PACOM.
       Sure enough, there are tourists there too—
       snapping like starved triggerfish. White-
       uniformed naval guides might be telling them how
              the USS *Arizona* was a 608-foot super dreadnought
              that now entombs 942 men. They might salute
              the dead soldiers, and ask for a moment of silence.
              They will not say the ship has been leaking
              2 to 9 quarts of oil every day for the past 75 years.
                     Or that since World War II the military has
                     stored its toxic waste in the harbor, where
                     it has leaked into groundwater wells. Or
                     that bunker fuel and other petroleum waste
                     have been leaking from a tank farm into
                     a 20-acre underground plume of 5 million gallons.

Or that mercury is in the soil. Or that pesticides, dry cleaning fluids,
and metal residues from the open burning of ordnances are in the soil.
Or that asbestos scrap, polychlorinated biphenyls, paints and solvents
are in the soil. Or tetrachloroethane and hydrocarbons in storm drains.
Or that there are 700 documented areas of contamination at Pearl Harbor.

Or that in 'Aiea, where we are close enough to hear
their 8 a.m. "Star-Spangled Banner" blare, our people are
walking, our children are playing. We are bathing and drinking.
We are driving and listening to NPR reports on defense spending.
We are watching reruns or DVR recordings of *NCIS* on TV.
We are eating and sleeping and breathing—and dying.

    And when they end the moment of silence
    for soldier sacrifice, they will salute their flag
    over Pu'uloa and her monstrous womb.

KŪPIKIPIKIʻŌ, OʻAHU

1.

Stand here, on the scarred edge
of this island, where Robert
Wilcox and Samuel Nowlein
would have stood in 1895
fighting to protect Hawaiʻi
from white annexationists
backed by the American military.
Here, where Hawaiʻi was annexed
without a treaty and in violation
of international law in 1898.
Stand at the jagged edge of 1916,
when Americans drilled and cracked
the reef and bombed coastal cliffs
to build battery after battery
for seacoast guns, reinforced
magazines for munitions,
and command bunkers before
decommissioning them all. Here,
where in 1933, Americans outfitted
a new battery with railway guns
and another magazine before
also decommissioning it. Stand
here, at the manicured edge
of a Black Point estate where
a tobacco heiress, once known
as the richest girl in the world,
built one of her mansions in 1937,
ornamenting her walls and floors
and courtyard with the art, jewels,
and prayers of Muslim people
whose countries, whose homes,
families, lands, and treasures

are bombed and shot by Americans
who bomb and burn and shoot Hawai'i
to train before leaving for combat.

2.

Stand here, at the top of Black Point,
one of the most exclusive places to live
in Hawai'i. Stand outside the outer
gate so you understand you don't belong
in any of their 75 lavish houses. You
have to imagine getting past that gate
and standing outside another—the inner
gate, the one that opens only for those
living in the 8 exclusive estates on Royal
Circle, named, as realtors say, because
only the highest of the Hawaiian chiefs
on O'ahu once lived there. You can only
stand at the secured edge of that land,
by the guard post, alone, since you'll never
have the financial portfolio to go in with
a global luxury realtor to tour the oceanfront
estate once owned by the original Magnum, P.I.
Tom Selleck (who now sells kūpuna reverse
mortgages) listed for $23 million or the Bali-
inspired villa for $14.8 million. You strain,
but can't see where those Americans stand safely
on their cliffside koa decks over the buried batteries
of war watching the distant waves rise and break.

3.

Stand here, at the breaking edge
of Iraq, Iran, and Afghanistan
as the American military invades
and raids their oil fields, as the U.S.
chooses their leaders and builds
Middle Eastern bases. Stand here,

as U.S.-backed regimes fall once
U.S. troops leave, as Afghan families
flee to crowded planes, closed borders.
Stand at the sharp edge of Raqqa,
Syria, where 300,000 people once lived,
where the U.S. dropped 10,000 bombs
and destroyed 80% of the city
through air strikes alone. Stand here,
at the receding edge of Palestine,
as Israel fires U.S. weapons to steal
family homes, whole communities, to build
military outposts, then Israeli settlements.
Stand here, on stolen land, at the edge of
fences, checkpoints, and guard posts.
Stand where international law is broken
without consequences. Stand at the edge
of hotels and mansions, military golf courses
over ancestral graves, adverse possession
and deeds from British or French mandate,
Israeli or American settlement and military
base, from overthrow and annexation,
from population transfer, from refugees
in exile left to wander the ruins hungry.

4.

Stand here, at the edge of return,
return to our people whose blood
and flesh and bone and hair, whose
roots and seeds have been ground
into the mud, the sand, held in black
basalt—we, the mauna, moana, ʻāina,
ʻikena—jabal, muhit, ʻard, almaerifuh.
Stand beside us where we breathe life
into ashes and become simurgh,
ʻalae. Where we return from flight,
from bomb and blood, from char
and exile. Where we return as rain

and salt, as eroding winds, as these
waves, as olive groves and orange
trees growing wild as vines of maile.
Stand with us where our lands are
returned and we returned to them.

5.

But first, stand at the edge of truth:

*This is not the United States. This is not a Christian state. This
is not the land of the free. This is not a papal bull. This is not
a U.S.-backed regime.*

This is Hawai'i. Kaho'olawe. Pōhakūloa.
Mākua. Kapūkaki. This is Guåhan. Litekyan. This is Samoa. This is
Puerto Rico. Vieques. This is the Marianas. Pagan. This is the Marshall
Islands. Bikini. Enewetak. Rongelap. This is the Federated States
of Micronesia. This is Palau. This is Turtle Island. This is Indian
Country. This is Palestine. This is Afghanistan. It is Iraq. It is Iran.
It is Syria. This is Okinawa. This is South Korea. Jeju.

*This is not
paradise. Not virgin land. Not real estate. Not wasteland. Not
your sacrifice or war zone. Not your American lake or wake. Not
your Pacific Pivot. Not your RIMPAC ocean. Not your vacation.*
This is stolen land and ocean. This is ancestor and descendant.

This is not Diamond Head.

This is Le'ahi.

This is not Black Point.

This is Kūpikipiki'ō.

Stand here.
Stand here.

WAIKĪKĪ ON GOOGLE MAPS
(SATELLITE VIEW)

In Waikīkī
Liliʻuokalani is just
a few blocks
from the
Royal Hawaiian
Shopping Center
and runs mauka
from Kalākaua
to the Ala Wai.

Kūhiō meets with her
amid vacation condos,
hotels, fenced empty lots
with tarped shopping carts,
overpriced apartments,
and ABC Stores,

as does Koa,
Prince Edward,
Cleghorn, and
Paoakalani.

Kaʻiulani parallels her
and runs mauka
but has a much
shorter life
before becoming
Kānekapōlei.

From Liliʻuokalani,

take Cleghorn,
Kūhiō, or Prince Edward
to the Princess Ka'iulani
Hotel.

When you get
to the King's Village
you must run
mauka with them
(but only to the Ala Wai)

and search
the brown canal water
for any part of us
that is still ours,

whatever remains
after even the names
of our kings and queens
have been taken,
left on the streets.

POSTCARDS FROM WAIKĪKĪ

for Westlake

*

Wish you were here in
Paradise, sipping mai tais
or something like that.

It's only gotten
worse—even more pigs and less
slop to go around.

*

You probably knew
the old pipes couldn't contain
all the shit of empire.

Two died—a tourist
and a military man
(who else goes to Waiks?)—

after falling in
the Ala Wai, pulsing with
staphylococcus.

(E Waikīkī 'ē,
spouting water spouts again—
the swamp thing's revenge!)

Not one janitor
could be found in all the land
except the ocean.

They still pay extra
for Diamond Head ocean views,

waves now barely brown.

*

I imagine you
with your kahuna
on the beach watching

pig oil make rainbows
on the water, imported
sand crusting your hand.

A dollar blows by,
then another, and no one
sees, or even cares.

Too little to be
worth chasing where there is too much
to regret, forget.

*

Wayne—can I call you
Wayne? No disrespect. You're more
a friend than uncle—

maybe it's better
to wish you weren't here to see
how it's even worse

than you remember:
more shit than the fake state
can hide in its dirty alleys.

Make yourself reborn
in the voice of leaves, raindrops,
sweep through these sidewalks.

Not even a light,
falling rain, warm to the spine,
can make us clean now.

LAST CORAL STANDING

me ka mahalo, after a painting by Joy Lehuanani Enomoto

You paint an ocean background,
lightening blues and grays. Emptied
of all life, all other color, so the polyps
expelled from their coral crevices
are held in that moment
right before death,
overheated and exposed.

You show us there is a kind
of beauty in their dying, in the way
their vessels constellate
in branches to echo the blood
in our veins, before
the salt water dissipates every
memory of their being.

But you urge us to remember
there is a brighter beauty in living:
Hānau ka pō
Hānau Kumulipo i ka pō, he kāne
Hānau Pōʻele i ka pō, he wahine
Hānau ka uku koʻakoʻa,
hānau kana, he ʻākoʻakoʻa, puka
We know coral polyps, living
in their perforated skeletal branches,
are our eldest kūpuna—What family
do we lose when the turning heat
reclaims them? What salt water
will rise in us, in that moment,
expelling blood from bone? Who
will still be here to remember that
we, temporary in such temperatures,
too, were beautiful once?

HE MELE ALOHA NO KA NIU

I'm so tired of pretending
each gesture is meaningless,

that the clattering of niu leaves
and the guttural call of birds

overhead say nothing.
There are reasons why

the lichen and moss kākau
the niu's bark, why

this tree has worn
an unseen ahu of ua and lā

since birth. Scars were carved
into its trunk to record

the moʻolelo of its being
by the passage of insects

becoming one to move
the earth speck by speck.

Try and tell them to let go
of the niu rings marking

each passing year, to abandon
their only home and move on.

I can't pretend there is
no memory held

in the dried coconut hat,
the star ornament, the midrib

bent and dangling away
from the root, no thought

behind the kāwelewele
that continues to hold us

steady. There was a time
before they were bent

under their need to make
an honest living, when

each frond was bound
by its life to another

like a long, erect fish
skimming the surface

of a sea of grass and sand.
Eventually, it knew it would rise

higher, its flower would emerge
gold, then darken in the sun,

that its fruit would fall, only
to ripen before its brown fronds

bent naturally under the weight
of such memory, back toward

the trunk to drop to the sand,
back to its beginnings, again.

Let this be enough to feed us,

to remember: ka wailewa

i loko, that our own bodies
are buoyant when they bend

and fall, that the ocean
shall carry us and weave us

back into the sand's fabric,
that the moʻopuna taste our sweet.

NĀ PU'U ONE O WAIHE'E

for Haumea and all the kupa'āina, aloha 'āina, and kia'i of Waihe'e

I.

You are still here—
the birthplace of salt
and wind, of rounded black
and red basalt pebbles, glittering
olivine, smoothed coral and bone.
The waves roll rock and reef,
tangled nets, tarp, plastic
bits cut and culled from
convenience, dulled
glass shards of
broken bottles.
Everything comes
to you freed from what
it once was, newly emerged—
to become the sand
in these dunes,
to live again.

2.

They say
before the drains
and grates that steal
the water of the valley,
lo'i kalo lehua lined the
stream banks, their leaves
and stalks trembling, young 'i'o
pounded for the throat-moistening
lehua poi. Your springs still gurgle up

through the wide archaeology
of your iwikuamoʻo to nurse
ʻūlei, hau, loulu, kauila
kiliʻoʻopu, naupaka,
ʻukiʻuki, pōhuehue,
ʻuhaloa, hōʻawa, kāwaʻu,
manono, kaluhā—all unfurl, weave
their roots, cling to the sands of Mauna
ʻIhi, even as the salt-wind bruises
their leaves, encrusts them, even
as the sun and salt desiccate
and sting, even as we all
may drift toward such
flight—then your water
upwells from below
bringing such
sweetness to
the loko
wai, the
muliwai.

3.

Aloha Waiheʻe
i ka makani paʻakai,
aloha nā makani e noho mau,
aloha e ʻAhaʻaha, aloha e ʻAkipohe,
aloha e Kiliʻoʻopu, aloha nō e ʻOʻopu.
Nip and waft, carrying rain
mist along the kahawai,
above hīhīwai, ʻōpae, nāpili
and nākea, blowing billows of sea
spray along the lei of dunes,
the hidden smoke of ʻoʻopu
long past but also

waiting.

Aloha Waiheʻe i ka ua
ānuenue, ke ao, ke ao akua,
ke aokū, ke ao loa, ke ao ʻōnohi,
aloha nō e ʻAkipohe, aloha
nō e Kiliʻoʻopu. Circle
and fall gently, then
thunder, upwell
the kahawai
until full,
flowing
freely
again.

4.

Aloha nō
e Haumea ē,
nui ka mahalo
for all you birthed,
shaped, and heaped from
reef, from mauna, from pali
from the ocean floor, all you eroded
carved from ice, wind, and rain,
from shell, coral, basalt and
bone to bring us
Mauna ʻIhi.

What is sand
but a return to life,
the brittle bones of before
breathing (birthing) again?
From you we know birth
to be just one of many
passages, that we
are born a flicker
of sun, emerge

a faint spark
or drop,
only the frailest
slivers from the branches
of Kalaukekahuli after it was
flung into the waves so
carelessly, that there
is pain and labor,
the stinging
salt of our sweat
and tears, our blood,
and it is how we learn
life is precious, remember
our histories, short and porous
as they are. Your pu'u one have a much
longer memory, have become a pewa binding
ocean to land, buffering storm surge,
offering moena makaloa of sand
and salt, cool springs from
underground tunnels that
hānai pools of loko wai,
ho'oipoipo with ocean
in the muliwai, where
underwater gardens
of limu, lacy black,
crunchy purple and red
fringed, and fat, juicy green
cling to the reef. Life begins again
as they hāpai warm nests, nurse new
hatchlings of ae'o, 'ua'u, and koloa, part
the grasses and sedge to reveal tender
caverns for piko and iwi. Your pu'u
are every beginning and every
return, waiwai of Waihe'e,
pu'u one hānau aloha.
Ho'i ke ola.
E ola nō.

'ehā

E lelehune nei
i ke one,
one hānau
o ke kupuna lā

hanau ponoi.   Aole like naka
ia ia mea he aloha ʻole ... hui
ke hoopaʻa, aʻ... hui ... ke
haha ia; aka, un... ...tu
oi... ... lele wale ... ...lu. i
kona ... ...aas ponoi iho, me
he u... ... 8... ...01 Meganeti.

Iau ... ... kui
hao Meganeti ... ... hookahi,
ai ala ... ...ropa ... me
... ...rokeramazo ... ...
iho iho ... iou ... ...kahi
...kahi.

... ...
... ...ho. ...huia ...
... ... aloha i... ...ua...i.
... ...menei ...ua ... ...hi ...i,
...a ...us. ... ...ho ...lehua kaohi
...h... ...ia ...iau ...on ... Laniakila
...eo... ... ...eu aina hanau.

O ke Aloha Aina, oia ka
Ume Makaneti iloko o ka huu-
wai o ka Lahui, o kaohi ana i
ke aloha Kuokoa, launakhi ana
o kona one hanau ponoi.

O ka Ume Makaneti, oia no
ka ikaika nana e kauo i ke kui
maganti o ka .... Kapo-
lulei ana i komo .... i ka
welelau. Akau o ka Hoailona,
a i ke hoku akau hoi.

.... pohihihi ka ike ana
i .... ana ai i ana he ume
iloko o ke .... i .... aka,
aia ka no .... a ..... e, aia
kela i .... hoomgu
ia .... konikuhi ana i ka
hoku akau ma ka welau akau o
honua nei.

Pela ke .... eu-
uwai o ke kanaka no kona aina

'ĀINA HĀNAU

for Kaikainali'i and Ku'uleihiwahiwa

I.

As it is told
there was darkness,
the deepest blackest
darkness called Pō,
turning in her sleep,
knowing what it is
not to breathe,
to verge between
need and climb.
He pō wale kēlā,
he pō wale kēia.

Her sleep was motherly,
thin and uneasy. She
dreamed of flying and falling.
Her turning churned
the dark to heat to light,
then to fire. She awoke
and gave birth first
to herself.
He pō wale kēlā,
he pō wale kēia.

The earth and heavens
turned hot and darkened.
Stars erupted on her
skin. Makaliʻi watched as
the walewale flowed
from her and welled
over it all and every
where and when
was breath.
He pō wale kēlā,
he pō wale kēia.

2.

Eia Hawai'i, he pae 'āina, he mau
moku, he mau kānaka, he mau
kānaka nui Hawai'i ē. He mau
Hawai'i kākou mau a mau.

Like you, these islands were born.
They came from Kāne, from Kū,
from Hina, from Lono, from Kanaloa,
from Haumea, from Papa, from Wākea,
from Ho'ohōkūkalani, from Kāulawahine,
from Lua, from Māui, from Pele, from
the deep darkness of Pō: Hawai'i,
Maui, Moloka'i, Lāna'i, O'ahu,
Kaua'i, Ni'ihau, Kaho'olawe.
They fed on water, salt, and heat,
crawled and then stood up in the light.
They grew tall and wide and turned
and slept and laughed and ate and
fought and shared in black and brown
and green and red. They inhaled earth
and exhaled mountains, beaches, pali,
and pōhaku. They inhaled sky, exhaled
the rains, winds, clouds, and stars.

Like you, these islands were born,
and every part of them born. Coral
children, worm children, shell, fish,
limu, grass, gourd, ocean, and forest
children. Children of rock and vine
and shrub and tree, fruit and fur.
Water children of salt and spring.
Insect children. Seeded, propagated,
corm children. Children who slither,
crawl, cling, and creep, who curl and unfurl,
who hatch, peck, bite, glide, and fly.

Rooting, digging, hill-building
children. Hiding, peeping, nesting
children. Brindled, speckled, tentacled
shape-shifters. Those with eight legs,
with eight eyes, those with four
and two. Those with fins, with iwi
and without. Tasters who sing
their names, and hearers who
answer or retreat. Children of howl
and screech, of paw and claw,
blind and sighted, tail and tendril,
skin and scale, web and wing,
stemmed, veined, and rooted.
Children o ke au iki a ke au nui.
ʻO nā mea ʻike maka ʻia,
ʻo nā mea ʻike maka ʻole.

Older, wiser children born
breathing long before us. Born
like you. Like these islands.

3.

Born are moʻolelo, seeds
strewn, the finest seeds
of stars in the heavens,
the seeds of gods. Born
from ocean, from spring,
from mountain, from pebble
and shell becoming sand.
Born from storm, from tide,
from crash and foam bubble.
Born from shoot, from leaf,
branch, from every body part,
from beyond the body, from
piko, from ʻaumākua,
from the darkness—born
from huli, from lewa, like you.

E hoʻolohe pono: every
moʻolelo is huli, every one
lewa between pō and ao,
lani and honua, mauka
and makai in the starred
salivary space, teeth
and tongue unleashed, pressed
through the pulse of clenched
jaw, quivering cheek, they
part pursed lips, voweling every
vestige of throat muscle, of larynx,
of diaphragmed breath, of naʻau—

puka mai ka moʻolelo,
hānau ka moʻolelo,
ua moʻolelo nō.

4.

As it is with moʻolelo,
there are always
many versions.

As it is told, Haumea
gives birth to mākua
from every part
of her body.

Papahānaumoku
gives birth to islands.

Hina gives birth to kapa,
to Māuiakamalo,
and to the reef and fish.

Hoʻohōkūkalani
gives birth to kalo
and the stars in his body.

Pele gives birth to fire,
smoke, and steam, then
to new black land.

Hiʻiaka gives birth to green,
to kupukupu, hāpuʻu, pālai,
ʻamaʻu, ʻēkaha, kīlau, niʻaniʻau,
pohole, pepeʻe, palahoʻa.

And there are more
mothers giving birth
to everything you see
and don't see. More
mothers giving birth
to bodies of water, of

words, of darkness, of
movement, of light. More
mothers feeding us safety,
shelter, love, beauty.

More mothers who have
always been from more
mothers. You should know
you have many mothers,
and you will be mothers
to many more.

5.

Another of our mothers
is Kahiki, her womb
a double-hulled wa'a
with thatched sails
like wings. In her, we
ate, slept, and breathed
salt water for months,
read currents of wind,
ocean, let ourselves
curl into waves when
heavy clouds darkened
the sky. All was ocean
and hollow sound on
the entering horizon.

The four stars
of Hānaiakamalama
turned, sank slowly
as Hōkūpa'a,
'Iwakeli'i, Nā Hiku
all floated higher
in the darkness
until Hōkūle'a.
Below us, dark wings
glided, filtering for limu.
Above us, moon-fade
flash of white wings
glided, circling for fish.

All we saw then
was Kānehoalani,
his fiery eye opening,
a ring of orange
and streaks of red.
We let the waves

carry us in, let
ourselves spill into
light—our islands
unfurling green.

6.

High in the mountains
in the piko of each
of these islands,
where earth sieves
the sky in the kua hiwi,
the kua mauna, the kua
lono, the kua hea,
the wao kele, the wao
akua, the wao lani,
where the air is
a thick howl and
the gods are seeds
of cold cloud mist
billowing between
short, bent trees—

na wai kēia moʻolelo hānau?

Descending to
the wao ʻeiwa,
the wao lipo, the
wao nahele,
the wao lāʻau,
where ʻōhiʻa, koa,
kukui, and ʻaʻaliʻi,
where māmane,
lauaʻe, wiliwili,
and ʻōhelo, where
alaheʻe, ʻūlei,
kauila, and maile,
where the uhiuhi,
kōkiʻo, ʻaiea, and
halapepe arouse
fat clouds with
sweetened wafts,

where the fog lingers
and drips and birds slurp,
their songs seeding
the understory—

na wai kēia moʻolelo hānau?

Flowing down
the ridges, over beds
of lipo, mossed
pōhaku, ʻiliʻili,
upwelling cool,
the gushing puna
of underground
arteries, from the
darkened blur of
cloud shadow
to the wao kanaka,
the wao ʻilima, the
wao ʻamaʻu, the kula,
where kalo, ʻuala,
ʻawa, wauke,
ʻulu, and maiʻa
flick and clatter
their leaves, and
tufts of tangled
pili ribs bow to
bury their seeds—

na wai kēia moʻolelo hānau?

Flowing still
to the muliwai,
where stream
and tide stir,
swirl, the murky
mouth, soil, salt,

and green gurgle
eddying brown,
mottled where
the seeds of moi,
āholehole, and
ʻamaʻama feed,
their dark spines
concealing as
they dive together,
channeling
current—

na wai kēia moʻolelo hānau?

7.

kūkulu: to build, as a house; pillar, post, side, border, edge, horizon; to construct, erect; to set up, as a hale frame; to heap up; to form; to found, as a society; to stand up together, as a multitude; with hale, *fig.*, to perpetuate a family; where the sky meets the horizon; nā kūkulu ʻehā: the four points of the compass; nā kūkulu o ka honua: the points or ends of the earth, that is, everywhere

papa: flat surface, stratum, plain, reef, layer, level, foundation, story of a building, floor; Native born, especially for several generations; set close together, thick together, as of growing plants, a thicket; in unison, all together; board, lumber; wooden

pou: post, pole, pillar, shaft; ridge, as of a nose; mast of a canoe; pouhana: two end posts, the tallest, their length the same as the hale's height; pouomanu: the center post; pou kaha or kihi: corner wall post; pou kukuna: end wall post; gate, door, or gable post

hāpai: to be pregnant with a child; to conceive; pregnancy; to carry, bear; to lift up, elevate, raise, hoist, hold up; to encourage or support, as another's testimony; to raise the hands, as in taking an oath; to honor; to praise; to exalt for past deeds; to recompense; to take up, that is, commence, as a speech; with pū, to act together

makuahine: mother, aunt, female cousin, or relative of the parents' generation; *lit.*, female parent; ʻōlelo makuahine: mother tongue; hoʻomakuahine: to act as or claim to be a makuahine; to treat as a makuahine

pūʻao: orifice of the womb; pū: conch shell, tree, head of octopus, squid, canoe end piece, coil of hair, topknot, to divide, to eat a little together, inactive, sluggish, entirely, completely, also with, together with; ʻao: a new shoot, leaf, or bud, especially of kalo

wahi ʻoiʻoi: tenon fashioned at the upper end and at the back of each pou; wahi: place, position, site, setting; ʻoiʻoi: full of sharp points, pointed, sharp; to protrude, stick, or jut out; also called ule

auwae: a curved notch cut on pou to form a protruding chin below the base of the wahi ʻoiʻoi on the back; used to connect pou to oʻa; also called kohe

kaupoku: the ridgepole, highest point, the roof, ceiling, attic; to set up a ridgepole; to thatch; *fig.*, greatest; also kaupaku: a partition; upper ridgepole, dividing the hale properly and acting as the bonnet or cap of the house

kuhikuhi puʻuone: seer, soothsayer, class of kahuna who advised on the building and location of temples, homes, fishponds; architectural engineer; *lit.*, point out the sand dunes

oʻa: rafters, roof beams; timbers in a ship's side; sides of a rock wall, gill of a fish; mouth of an eel

uli: early stage in the development of a fetus, as the body begins to form; any dark color, including the deep blue of the sea, the ordinary green of vegetation, and the dark of black clouds; to steer

mana: stage of the fetus in which limbs begin to develop; also kaha: stage in growth of fish when colors appear; power, authority; branch, limb

iwikuamoʻo: spine, backbone; near and trusted relative of a chief who attended to his/her/their needs and possessions, and executed private orders; family

pale keiki: to deliver a child; an obstetrician; a midwife; class of kahuna who advised ʻohana and wahine during pregnancy and through childbirth; *lit.*, shield the child

alawela: dark line that grows from the top of the abdomen and from the bottom of the abdomen of a pregnant woman (when the lines meet in the navel to form one line, the baby would be born) kua'iole: upper ridgepole of a hale, which secures the ends of the o'a to the kauhuhu; kua: back, rear, windward; to carry on the back, as a child; to hew, chop, chip, hack, strike, cut out; to fell, strike down; women's hale used for beating kapa; back side of a place; ma ke alo o kēia 'āina, he *kua* o ka moku 'ia; 'iole: mouse or rat

pohā ka nalu: breaking of the waters; pohā: to burst, crack, break forth, crash; to ferment (of poi); flashing of light, breaking of bubbles; nalu: wave, surf; full of waves; to form waves; amniotic fluid; to be in doubt or suspense; to wonder at; not to comprehend speech or language; to speak secretly, or to speak to one's self; to think to one's self

kauhuhu: a ridge or edge of a precipice; pole running lengthwise along a house to which the tops of the o'a are fastened; a ridgepole lying beneath the kua'iole of a house

nahunahu: to feel the first pains of childbirth; biting pain

lu'ukia: to lash with coconut fiber; various hale lashings including kauhihi, used to tie 'aho to pou; 'aho 'ōwili, used to fasten the kaupoku to the kua'iole; ki'ihei, used to secure lohelau to pou; and kauhilo, used to tie horizontal thatching sticks and plates

hāhā: to palpate or feel the body with the hands to diagnose sickness or to externally manipulate a baby in the womb into the correct position for birth, done by the pale keiki

kanaka kūkulu hale: builder of a hale; construction worker

ko'o kua: helper accompanying the pale keiki who sits behind the person in labor giving back support, and with arms wrapped tightly, presses down in the front during the bearing-down phase

'aho: purlin of a house; breath, to breathe; 'ahopi'o: thatch-support purlin to which layers of pili would be fastened; 'ahokele: horizontal purlin; 'ahopi'o kuahui: purlin support rod; 'ahopueo or ke'a: fixed purlin, main purlin

kōhi: to strain, especially as in childbirth; to gather, as fruit; to break off neatly, as a kalo corm from the stalk; to split, as breadfruit; to dig; fat, rich, as food; prolonged, as a sound; long

holo: diagonal pole or strut attached to the inner side of the roof frame and extending from the upper end of an o'a at one corner to the lower end of the o'a at the other corner; to run, sail, ride, go; to flow, as water; decided, determined, agreed upon, settled

'ina'ina: reddish evacuation preceding labor in childbirth; the mucus plug or bloody show. Ua hemo ka 'ina'ina o ke keiki, ua kokoke paha i ka manawa e hānau ai: The 'ina'ina has been discharged, so the time of birth is near.

pueo: hale lashing; ku'u manu noho pū me ke kanaka: pueo (riddle); my bird living with people; owl (pun on 'aho pueo and pueo for the hale)

kahi hāiki: birth canal; narrow place; aia nō i kahi hāiki: just there in a narrow place (said of an unborn child); ka hāiki o ka manawa: limitations of time; hā: a water trough; to breathe; iki: small

'uki'uki: native member of the lily family, with a short stem and long, narrow leaves, from among which arises a cluster of white or bluish flowers (its leaves were dried and braided to make lashings to tie 'aho)

hō'i'ī: to strain and grunt, as during childbirth or while enduring labor pains pili: long, coarse grass used to thatch hale, so called because of how the seeds detach from the stalk and stick to a person's clothes; preferred over other grasses for its fragrance and symbolism; shingles, so called because they replaced pili on the roofs of hale; to cling, stick, touch, join, be with; to agree

hauʻoki: medicine made of hau bark and given to those in labor to ease pain and to help increase the wale-wale so the infant can slide out; hau and ʻilima blossoms also used; hau:lowland tree with rounded heart-shaped leaves and flowers with five large petals that change through the day from yellow to dull-red; kinolau of Haumea; ʻoki: to cut, sever, or separate

niʻo: highest point, pinnacle; to reach the summit; doorway or threshold of a house; an altar; to be spotted or streaked; to sit in the doorway in an open door; to sit or sleep in an entranceway to protect one's hale

kuakoko: childbirth, bearing-down labor; the results of uncontrolled emotions; kua: the back of a person or animal in distinction from the face; the top of a ridge, or highland; var. of akua, god, image; the midrib; koko: blood; rainbow hued; the netting around a calabash; falling rain where the light shines through and it appears reddish

8.

Before first is cloud
edge thirst, is electric
current slither. Before
first thrums illiterate
in lethargic bloat.
But before first was
just fine to thirst,
slither, thrum, bloat
in darkness, to wait
to become—and well,
before first was
still *technically* first—
which is to tell you
you have to be
careful with firsts
since first is one
of many mothers
without memory of
the firsts before her.

What I mean
is there can be
more than one first:
It is true that Pō
was first, that first
was slime, the plant
people, the ocean
people, first, that
four, six, eight,
and more legged
people were first.
It is true Laʻilaʻi
was the first woman,
who brought forth
the ao with Kiʻi,

the first mahū,
and Kāne, the first
man. From them,
Kamahaʻina was
the first child. It is
also true that Papa
was the first woman,
who birthed the islands,
and Wākea, the first
man. It is true Hāloa
was the first child, but
stillborn and buried,
that from his grave,
the first kalo sprouted,
its leaves tall, stalks
trembling, its ʻiʻo
momona enough
to feed all the firsts
to come afterward.

What I mean
is we can never
really know enough,
so you have to be
careful with firsts.
ʻO ke akua ke komo
ʻaʻoe komo kanaka.
We are all always
firsts and before
firsts becoming,
bursting in form,
in new possibility.

9.

With you
my body was Pō,
some unknowable
dark dwelling full
and slow. The world
was water to you.
I hope it was heart-
beat and song too.

When you were
wing flutter, I slept
long and had dreams
of flying and falling
from where toward
where I don't know.

When you were
heleuma, turning
and sinking, my body
swelled and flooded.
Sleep was in waves.
I dreamed of my
father, who loved
the ocean, and woke
in sweat. On my skin,
silver rivulets zigzagged
like lightning from
my piko. A dark line
trickled down from
my heart and up from
beneath my belly, over
the whole of you,
the whole of me.

The world was water.

And heartbeat and
song. I was an opening
nuku, almost high
tide, a heavy heap
of cloud, full and still
somehow floating.

10.

Now I can
only tell you
what little I know
about darkness
about islands
about mothers
about water
about birth.

I can tell you
that when the time
came I did not need
to know about any
of it I just had to
let my body be
darkness
islands
mothers
water
to birth.

I had to move
toward darkness
I had to breathe islands
I had to rise mothers I had to
fall water I had to turn dark I had
to float islands I had mothers to breathe
water darkly I had to sink islands I had mothers
to lose water my body darker I had islands to breathe
mothers I had water to find darkening my body islands I
had to inhale mothers I had water to exhale darkness I had
island mothers to feel water I had dark island mothers to become
me I had water to darken islands to inhale mothers I had water dark
islands to exhale mothers I had water to forget darker me I had
islands to mother remember you I had to open water open

darkening islands to inhale mothers I had watered dark
islands to exhale mothers I had to open water to rise
darkened island mothers to open watered darkness
I had islands to open to fall mothers I had water
to let dark island mother water make me
darkness islands mothers water
strong inhale darkness so
islands exhale mothers so
water I had dark to open islands
mothers to open darkness to be stronger
than I knew islands mothers water I could ever
be I had to push with darkness islands mothers water
push so I could be darkness islands mothers water for you
push so all darkness for you all islands
push for you so all mothers for you
push all water for you   all for you

                                    all light for you

                                        for us to
                                        breathe.

II.

After it all, you came
into light, eyes open.
Your father caught you.
Your throat cleared,
you breathed. Your
father brought you to
my breast, you were
warmed, fed. You slept.

For you, kuʻu maka,
I floated full with thoughts
of who you would be.
Stars spilled premonitions
of your face, your voice.
But you have to be
careful with firsts, and so
I had been studying and
steadying, trying to
choose what was best,
what may have been
more like our kūpuna,
what natural birth books
and videos said could give
you optimal health, a less
traumatic birth. I had a doctor
who said I was *unfortunately*
geriatric, tracked my weight,
had me drink orange sugar
syrup to measure my insulin
response. Another doctor
screened for genetic diseases,
urged me to let them stab
a long needle in my womb
to screen for Down syndrome.
Another who said I may have

cervical cancer and wanted
to cut part of my cervix,
though it could hurt you.

I was told over and over
that my body was failing,
that I could be dying, that
I may be hurting you, that
you may be hurting me.
I hated them. I cried.
All the times I was so
sick as a child, struggling to
breathe, on IVs, stuck with
needles—my body exhausted
and at the mercy of men
in white coats or blue
scrubs, when one was able
to get me alone—it all came
back. I was older and stronger,
but afraid of being in a hospital
again, of needing to stop
someone, and being unable,
again, for both of us.

I was lost. I had long talks
with you. I sang to you.
I sang for you. I asked
our kūpuna, your grandfather,
for help. I found a doula,
then a midwife to help me.
I found home birth. I found
a birth class for ʻŌiwi
women. I found Haumea,
I found Papa, I found Pō.
I found ʻāina, I found aloha.
I sang to you. I sang for you.

And I found, when you
were born, our bodies were
strong—we were always
enough. Your breath
to my breast, we fed
and breathed together,
slept safe at home.

12.

I'm not sure where I first heard that 'Ōiwi women
do not scream when they hānau, that doing so would
be considered embarrassing or attention seeking.
I've never seen another 'Ōiwi woman hānau, not
even your aunties, and it never seemed appropriate
to ask. I can tell you, though, that when the time came
I didn't scream—not because I was worried I wouldn't
be 'Ōiwi enough if I did, or that somehow I'd bring
shame to my 'ohana (those kinds of self-conscious
thoughts don't really happen since your focus isn't
on what others might think of you)—but because
screaming seemed so loud and outward, and all I
wanted was to go inward. When you hānau, you stay
with your body, pulsing through every contraction, but
in the soft lull between the rise and fall of waves you find
hānau makes time stretch slippery tentacles to hold you
as you slide between pō and ao, not quite dreaming.

13.

You were in the dark waves
for a time, your body a pearl
of flesh, hands and feet formed,
ears, nasal passages, a tongue
and palate in your mouth.
Something in the dark called
and you followed, leaving
only your body to come
into light. You were wrapped
and held before you were buried.
You are loved and missed.

In this time, when your child
dies in your womb before birth,
an American medical doctor
will do an ultrasound. As you watch
the tiny blurred body on the screen
he'll tell you the fetus is no longer
viable, that you must decide—
D&C (dilation and curettage)
or wait to miscarry at home.
He will explain D&C involves
dilating your cervix and then
scraping and suctioning the fetus
and placental tissues out of you.
He will say that if you wait
for your body to miscarry, it could
take weeks and will be painful
and messy. You feel very alone.
You think of all the ways you
caused this, how your body—how
you—failed because you miscarried.
You try not to tell anyone
because you don't want them
to say it was probably for the

best or at least you weren't
that far along or that you need
to just let it go. In another time,
you would have had ʻohana
around you who knew what to say
and do to help you. A Hawaiian
medical doctor would hāhā
your ʻōpū as you described what
happened and tell you *he keiki*
heʻe wale or *he keiki hāʻule wale*,
yours is a child who will flow
away, a child who will fall like rain.
You would be given tea to drink
and time to grieve, pray, reflect,
and dream, and you and your ʻohana
would be asked to share feelings
to heal you, and when it was time
for your keiki to flow from your body,
your keiki would be wrapped in kapa
and planted as songs fell like rain.

We tried our best to give that to you,
kuʻu keiki aloha. You sank down from us
like water, our love for you loosening
the earth beneath the lauaʻe, its cradling roots.

14.

hale: house, building; sheltered
and enclosed place; a hospitable
person, host. 'Ohana had 6 or more
hale: a heiau for worship; a mua
for men's eating; a noa, where all of
the 'ohana could be together freely;
an aina for women's eating; a kua,
where women beat kapa; and a pe'a
for women during menstruation
and childbirth. A separate hale
moe could also be included for the
'ohana to sleep in, though without
one, everyone slept in the hale noa.

'ale'o: a garret sometimes made in
the upper part of the hale, used to
store treasures, weapons, and heir-
looms; a high lookout; towering
above; nā pali 'ale'o, towering cliffs

halake'a: upright posts within the
hale to which la'aukea, or crossties,
were fastened

keiki: little one, child, youngster,
no matter which gender; offspring,
whether a child or grown person;
progeny, descendant of any number of
degrees; also the young of animals or
plants, such as a shoot of kalo; keiki
hānau o ka 'āina: a native child, one
born of the land

'iewe: afterbirth; placenta; an infant,
a young one just born; relatives of a
common ancestry. E kolo ana nō ka
ēwe i ka 'iewe: descendants of the
same kūpuna find one another.

ēwe: navel string, mature birth;
sprout, rootlet; lineage, kin; birth-
place; family trait; to sprout; ēwe
hānau o ka 'āina: Natives of the land;
i ke ēwe 'āina o ke kupuna, in the
ancestral homeland

piko: long thatch of pili hung over to cover the door of a new hale that was ready for habitation (the thatch was cut by a kahuna in a ceremony to oki ana o ka piko o ka hale—to cut the hale's piko—as one would do with a newly born baby); summit or top of a hill or mountain; crest; end of a rope; a center

piko: navel, navel string, umbilical cord; *fig.*, blood relative, genitals; crown of the head; small wauke rootlets from an old plant; place where a stem is attached to the leaf, as of taro; also hāwele: *fig.*, umbilical cord

lohelau: wall; wall plate; lohe: to hear, mind, obey, listen; to feel, as the tug of a fishing line; lau: leaf, frond, leaflet, greens; to leaf out; sheet; surface; blade, as of grass; to be much, many; very many, numerous

kilo: to watch closely, examine, look around, observe, forecast, as in a child's purpose; to look earnestly; a stargazer, reader of omens, seer, astrologer; to watch omens; to give heed to signs in order to forecast events; to watch or look for the purpose of discovering; to glean; to gather what remains in the soil after the crop is removed

puka: door, entrance to a hale (the main door was in the middle of the front, a smaller door at the rear); to pass through, appear, emerge; to enter or pass through a hole, crevice, or doorway; to rise, as the sun or as a subject, to usurp the authority of a ruler; to pass from one state or condition to that of another

hānau: to give birth; to lay (an egg); born; offspring, child, childbirth; to be productive, fertile; 'ili'ili hānau: pebbles that can reproduce; welo hānau: a productive or prolific family; to come from or be separated, as a young animal from its mother; to be born; to bring forth, as a mother; baptism

'eleua: a new house before it has been made noa; smaller door at the rear of the hale; dark rain or full rain clouds; a kupuna, especially kupunakāne of an 'ohana

'uki'uki: plant producing fruits that are blue berries, which are boiled and used to dye kapa (the dye is a grayish blue; a kapa used to catch a baby who was just born was dyed blue with 'uki'uki)

kuwā: prayer for special events, as cutting the piko of the hale, or completion of a new canoe or net

kāle'a: prayer calling on the 'aumākua, family gods, for help; to pray thus

kū'ono: nook, cranny, interior of a house opposite the door, inside corner of a house; gulf, bay, indentation, cell (of a beehive); 'a'ohe mea koe ma kū'ono: nothing left in the corners (of a generous person); deep, as a cave; deep down, profound

pueo: to rock an infant on the foot (while doing this, one amused the child by chanting pūeoeo); owl; he manu lele hihiu (the pueo is one of the po'e akua mana); keiki a ka pueo: child of the owl (one whose father is not known)

kala: gables, the ends of a house, the portion of the wall between the edges of intersecting roof pitches; same as hākala; also, to loosen and free, to forgive, pardon, or excuse, to release, unburden, absolve, so as to let go of kaumaha; to ho'omāmā; 'O ke kala 'ana kekahi ala o ke ola. 'O kekahi ala o ke ola. E hāhai i nā ala i kou hale maluhia.

ho'oleilei: to swing a baby so as to soothe or entertain; to juggle; to wear a lei or leis; lei: a garland or wreath of flowers; *fig.*, a well-loved keiki, so called since the keiki's arms went round the neck like a lei as the makua or kupuna carried the keiki; also said to be because the keiki would be carried on the shoulders and their legs would hang on both sides of the makua or kupuna like a lei; keiki are the most precious lei

15.

After it all, you came
into light, eyes open.
Your throat cleared,
you breathed. You
were brought to my
breast, you were
warmed, you fed,
squeezed my finger.
Your father cut
your piko. You slept.

For you, ku'u hi'ilei,
I knew more, but each birth
is different. I was careful
with you, guarded. I miscarried
at 11 weeks the year before.
We were 14 weeks along
before I told anyone except
your father about you, but
I talked to you, sang to you,
asked you to be strong. I studied
and steadied, like with Sister,
I rubbed my 'ōpū with kukui oil,
went for walks. I tracked my own
glucose, ate poi, limu, lū'au, eggs
and fish, refused the orange sugar
syrup, recorded everything I ate.
When the doctor and nurse said
no one has ever refused, I fed them
logs and charts, said they could
label me overweight and diabetic,
but I would not drink it. They left it
up to other doctors, who I also fed
logs and charts, and who, after
several weeks, were finally full.

It was a small victory, if you can
even call it that, but it was
the first time I felt my decisions
for our bodies were respected.

Like before with your sister,
it was all so patriarchal and
colonial. I wanted to be closer
to our kūpunahine, so I learned
how to kuku kapa from Aunty L.
I bought a kua, hohoa, and
iʻe kuku from Aunty D. One
of my haumana, Aunty A,
joined us to learn too. We
three ʻŌiwi women went
to the wauke, with permission
from Aunty M and Uncle K,
offering our oli to Mānoa
and Kāneʻohe. We stripped
the stalks and soaked the white
inner bark. After a week, we
met again, sang our oli to
Kānehoalani, then began,
our voices quiet, as the music
ʻouʻou, ʻouʻou, ʻouʻou, ʻouʻou,
wood against raw cloth, water
and wood echoed, until white
sheets of kapa flowed out,
wet and thin, and our arms
and shoulders ached. You
were there, sloshing waves
inside me. A few weeks later,
when I was nearly 36 weeks,
my water leaked. Grandma
stayed with Sister, and we went
to the hospital, where we were
told we needed to induce labor

early. The doctors and nurses
inserted IVs in me, taped sensors
to my ʻōpū to hear your heartbeat
and to monitor my vitals. Your
father and I went over our birth
plan. They started the Pitocin,
and I repeated that I did not
want an epidural. I tried not
to be afraid of you being early,
of feeling everything more
intensely. Your father and I were
mostly alone, counting between
contractions, waiting. I told him
to remind me that each time
was only going to be a minute
and that each time would bring
me closer to you. Just before
the last contraction, I felt you
drop down inside me. There were
other rooms with other women
in labor and so the nurse had told
me not to push, but my body
and you took over. Your father
screamed for the doctor, who came
but had only seconds to put
on his mask and gloves before
you were born in one big push.

16.

E kuʻu mau ʻōmaka i ke kīhāpai:
may you always know these islands,
like you, Daughters, are more
than enough, know that like you,
they are everything beautiful,
everything buoyant. Their winds
and rains and mountains, ravines
and valleys love without question.
Like our islands, may you give birth
first to yourselves, then love always
with green tenderness, thrusting
your hands into mud, opening
your body into ocean, knowing
these islands are here for you,
for your children and their children,
knowing we *are* these islands.

For you, may there always be refuge,
safety within the walls you reach,
behind borders, under flags, and in
your own bodies. May you always
be grateful for peace, for open harbors
not freely entered, for treaties honored,
for nothing taken that was not first
given, for iwi still earthed, for new
coral growth unbleached, for black
cloud cover and trees, breathable air,
a beach, stream, or ocean without
plastic tangle or sewage or toxic seep.

I wish you words and medicines
that lift and heal, vegetables and fruit
from organic earth, free-flowing waters
from mountain to ocean, Daughters, cool
and clean, unowned, shared. I wish you

ocean-salted rocks and shells you can taste
and hold in your mouth, blades of grass
and ridged bark—all coolness and warmth
to press to your cheek, to your lips. May you
know love in every form, but always
in the food you eat, that you love the crust
dried poi makes on the skin around your lips,
the dark green of lūʻau, soft steam of ʻulu,
of ʻuala, the way you must slurp the red wild
of ʻōhiʻa ʻai—all from ʻāina you've curled
your toes into—may you always be full.

May there be hiding places to keep you
as hidden as you want, climbing places
to keep you above, flying places, resting
places, low-lying and high-cliff caves,
more places carved by winds and rains,
salt and waves, fragrant jungles, terraced
gardens, islands old and still being born,
places where you wait for welcome,
places that you know are not for you
or anyone to enter—may you protect all
of those places and may they protect you.

May the wind and waves lift you up
and may you let yourself fly, wonder,
from a pali overlook as ʻiwa or pueo
circle above, or as koholā or naiʻa
breach through ocean in the distance,
about lightness and sky—that you
remember you can rise high above
whatever may hold you down.

May you hear these islands breathe
with you, let them be big enough
to carry you, small enough to carry
with you. May you know these islands

depend on your breath, that the ocean,
rains, and winds need your voice.
That every green growing thing lives
and births more green growing.
That there is safety and warmth
enough, shade enough when you
need it—water, food, shelter, love.
That you sleep deeply and
let yourself hear our kūpuna.

May you know smallness—know
to be careful and think of unseen
workings, to remember the smallest
can be the strongest, to feel you are
islands like ours, not separated
by ocean—but threaded—your roots
woven and fed by the same fire
and water and salt and darkness.

May you know immensity too—
that even when you think you are
alone, that you feel the ocean
in your sweat and tears, that you
watch rain wash the hillsides
into a dark stream and see your skin,
that the sun, moon, and stars, dark
underwater caverns, underground rivers,
all you see and don't see of ʻāina,
are your kūpuna, your ʻohana in
your every breath, that something
of you, something of all of us before,
and something of all of us to come
are these islands. May this always
be with you: e ola mau, e ola nō.

NUI KE ALOHA ME KA MAHALO (ACKNOWLEDGMENTS)

FOR THE 'āina who raised, sheltered, and taught me—Haleakalā, Pulehunui, A'apueo, Kapālama, Mānoa, Makiki, 'Aiea, me Kalaepōhaku.

For nā akua me nā kupuna, whose mana and divine interventions make everything possible.

For all of our older, wiser nonhuman relatives.

For my kūpuna (Leinā'ala and Clifford Kekauoha, Normalee and Paul McDougall), my mākua (Laura Lei Kekauoha and Jeffrey McDougall), my many mana wahine 'anakē (Stacy Ching, Carolyn Nani-Jill Azbell, Robin DeCoite, Lynn Arce, Alexa Tim, and lucky for me, so many, many more!), my kaikaina (Janelle McDougall-Shaw, Cherie Ku'ikalono Hoshino, and Dawn Hālona Hoshino), my hoa hānau (Taylor Ching, Ke'ala Ching, Katie McDougall, and also lucky for me so many more!), all my nieces and nephews, and all the rest of my 'ohana for your aloha, kāko'o, mo'olelo, malu, and mana.

For my kumu makamae for your lessons and generosity—Renee Adams, Rama Camarillo, Healani Huch, Russ Martin, Jim Slagel, Kāwika Makanani, Donald Dorr-Bremme, Garrett Hongo, Albert Wendt, Reina Whaitiri, Witi Ihimaera, Jim Henry, Cristina Bacchilega, Laura Lyons, Robert Sullivan, Noenoe Silva, Haunani-Kay Trask, David Stannard, Allison Adelle Hedge Coke, and Joy Harjo.

For the contemporary 'Ōiwi writers before me who have been lighting the path of poetry, publishing, and activism, especially John Dominis Holt, Leialoha

Perkins, Joe Balaz, Imaikalani Kalahele, Puanani Burgess, Haunani-Kay Trask, Wayne Kaumualii Westlake, Māhealani Perez-Wendt, Dana Naone Hall, Victoria Nālani Kneubuhl, Māhealani Dudoit, and kuʻualoha hoʻomanawanui (kaikuaʻana kine).

For my Maui tita Joy Lehuanani Enomoto, for your inspiring activism and insight and for your stunning and intricate artwork, *Journey of the Blue Jellyfish*, which graces the cover of this book, and for your generous gifts of art, laughter, wit, and friendship over the years.

For Allison Leialoha Milham for your aloha ʻāina, friendship, and talent and for the gorgeous and thoughtful art-maps (ʻohana portraits) and sumi ink ʻāinascapes you created for the dividing pages of this book.

For all of the talented and supportive folks at the University of Arizona Press, especially Elizabeth Honor Wilder, Julia Balestracci, Leigh McDonald, Mari Herreras, Abby Mogollón, Amanda Krause, and to Marie Landau for her careful and thoughtful copyediting. Mahalo nui to Ofelia Zepeda and the editorial board of the Sun Tracks series for your leadership and for bringing so many beautiful Indigenous books to us. Honored to have this book as part of the series.

For kuʻu kupunahine ʻo Leināʻala Goodness Kekauoha, kuʻu makuahine ʻo Laura Lei Kekauoha, Georganne Nordstrom, Herve Collin, Cristina Bacchilega, Lynn Arce, Alexa Tim, Areerat Worawongwasu, Vernadette Gonzalez, Lani Teves, Joy Enomoto, and Allison Hedge Coke, Hazel, and the rest of the Hedge Coke ʻohana, Diana Fontaine, and Nicole and Sophia Furtado for being there for me with aloha nui, moʻolelo, kamaʻilio, and kākoʻo.

For Craig Santos Perez for your support and for our beautiful children.

For my kamaliʻi Kaikainaliʻi and Kuʻuleihiwahiwa—mahalo piha for all of the sweetness, silliness, strength, determination, curiosity, beauty, intelligence, joy, and love you share and bring into my life. You inspire me in countless ways every day.

For the amazing, vibrant, and supportive literary community in Hawaiʻi and throughout the Pacific, especially Noʻu Revilla, Kai Gaspar, kuʻualoha hoʻomanawanui, Aiko Yamashiro, Bryan Kamaoli Kuwada, Hailiʻopua Baker, Kaliko Baker, Lyz Soto, Emelihter Kihleng, Grace Iwashita-Taylor, Marie Alohalani Brown, Meredith Desha Enos, Donovan Kūhiō Colleps, Heoli Osorio, David Kealiʻi MacKenzie, Dan Taulapapa McMullin, Rajiv Mohabir, Kapulani Landgraf, leilani portillo, and Kristiana Kahakauila, and for our new poets emerging.

For the Disability Justice Hui—Halena Kapuni-Reynolds, Aree Worawong-wasu, Māhealani Ahia, Kahala Johnson, Pōmaikaʻi Gushiken, Katherine Achacoso, Leiana Nāholowaʻa, and Sandra Yellowhorse (and awesome, beautiful Tifa!). Nui ke aloha me ka mahalo for your beauty, strength, thoughtfulness, and brilliance, for our collective synergy of manaʻo and naʻau, and for all the ways we are growing and healing.

For all the folks who worked to create and build the Hawaiʻi State Poet Laureate Program, namely the Hawaiʻi Council for the Humanities (especially Aiko Yamashiro, Lyz Soto, and Rob Chang), the Hawaiʻi State Foundation on Culture and the Arts (especially Kacey Bejado), and the Hawaiʻi State Public Library System (especially Stacey Aldrich), and to the inspirational poet Kealoha for forging such a beautiful path to follow. Mahalo also to Senator Brian Taniguchi and Representative Cedric Gates for sponsoring the Hawaiʻi Poet Laureate resolution.

For all of my haumāna, for your hope, wisdom, energy, and aloha. Mahalo piha for all you teach me.

For all the Indigenous, Pacific, Black, Asian, Latinx, queer, disabled, and womyn poet-warriors, artists, anticolonial activists, truth tellers, birthing bodies, and survivors—you're all relatives, whether we've met yet or not. Let's keep creating and growing until we remake all spaces as healing spaces.

For the aloha ʻāina and kākoʻo who kūʻē in big and small ways to protect the ʻohana, kaiāulu, and ʻāina of our islands.

For the ēwe hānau o ka ʻāina who have enduring aloha nui for our ʻāina hānau. Ua mau ke ea o ka ʻāina i ka pono.

◆

"Real (G)estate" was created with the help and support of Allison Adelle Hedge Coke, Hazel Hedge Coke, and Nicole Furtado. Section 2 of "Real (G)estate" is forthcoming in an as yet untitled anthology edited by Franny Choi, Noʻu Revilla, Terisa Siagatonu, and Bao Phi.

"Nā Puʻu One o Waiheʻe" appeared in *Writing the Land: Windblown II*, edited by Lis McLoughlin (NatureCulture, 2022). With special mahalo to the Hawaiʻi Island Land Trust.

"The Map" appeared in *About Place Journal* (Volume VII, Issue I: "Navigations: A Place for Peace," edited by Allison Adelle Hedge Coke, May 2022). With mahalo nui for a Pushcart nomination.

"Water Remembers" appeared, under a slightly different title, in *Water Lore: Practice, Place and Poetics*, edited by Claudia Egerer and Camille Roulière (Routledge, 2022).

"ʻĀina Hānau" and "Puʻuloa" appeared in *Bamboo Ridge* (Issue 119, "Kīpuka: Finding Refuge in Times of Change," edited by Donald Carreira Ching, Meredith Desha Enos, Brenda Kwon, and Misty-Lynn Sanico, October 2021). "ʻĀina Hānau" also appeared in *The Fantastic in Oceania*, edited by Cristina Bacchilega, kuʻualoha hoʻomanawanui, and Joyce Pualani Warren (University of Hawaiʻi Press, forthcoming). "Puʻuloa" was also performed at Songs at the Confluence: Indigenous Poets on Place, A Digital Poetry Event hosted by Tippet Rise Art Center and Adrian Brinkerhoff Poetry Foundation (livestreamed and launched December 4, 2020).

"This Island on Which I Love You" appeared in *Living Nations, Living Words: An Anthology of First Peoples Poetry*, edited by Joy Harjo (W. W. Norton, 2021). It also appeared in "Living Nations, Living Words: A Map of First Peoples Poetry," signature project of Joy Harjo, 23rd Poet Laureate of the United States (Library of Congress, launched November 2020), and in *New Poets of Native Nations*, edited by Heid E. Erdrich (Graywolf Press, 2018). This poem was inspired by and draws from some of the rhetoric of Li-Young Lee's "The City in Which I Love You."

"Kūpikipikiʻō, Oʻahu" and "Resist" appeared as an 8x8 exhibition at the Shangri-La Museum of Islamic Art, Culture, and Design (launched December 18, 2020). With special mahalo nui to Karima Daoudi, Kristin Remington, and Navid Najafi (Illnomadic). "Resist" also appeared in the Poem-a-Day series, edited by R. Erica Doyle (Academy of American Poets, July 2021).

"Kūpikipikiʻō" was an April 2023 National poetry month selection of *The Rumpus* edited by Cortney Lamar Charleston.

"Poem for the Cancel RIMPAC Coalition" is a collaborative poem whose other contributors are Emalani Case, Grace Iwashita-Taylor, D. Kealiʻi MacKenzie, Emelihter Kihleng, Bobbie Millar, Billy Kinney, A. A. Hedge Coke, Nadine Anne Hura, Tāwhana Chadwick, Kisha Borja-Quichocho-Calvo, Jamaica Heolimeleikalani Osorio, and Loke Aloua. It was recorded in a video directed and edited by Mikey Inouye, and produced by Emalani Case, Joy Enomoto, and Mikey Inouye (released on YouTube, July 2020).

"He Mele Aloha no ka Niu" appeared in *When the Light of the World Was Subdued, Our Songs Came Through: A Norton Anthology of Native Nations Poetry*, edited by Joy Harjo, with LeAnne Howe, Jennifer Foerster, and contributing editors (W. W. Norton, 2020), and in *POETRY* (July/August 2016).

"Haleakalā on Google Maps (Satellite View)," "Kūkaʻōʻō Heiau on Google Maps (Satellite View)," "The King Kamehameha Statue on Google Maps (Map View)," "Honokāhua on Google Maps (Satellite Then Street Then Satellite View)," and "Waikīkī on Google Maps (Satellite View)" appeared, under slightly different titles, as part of the chapter "Finding Direction: Google Mapping the Sacred, Moʻolelo Mapping Wahi Pana in Five Poems" in *Detours: A Decolonial Guide to Hawaiʻi*, edited by Hōkūlani Aikau and Vernadette Vicuña Gonzalez (Duke University Press, 2019). "King Kamehameha," "Kūkaʻōʻō Heiau," and "Waikīkī" also appeared in *Black Renaissance/Renaissance Noire* (Volume 13, Issue 1, June 2013).

"American Poem," and "The Kahului McDonald's" appeared in *New Poets of Native Nations*, edited by Heid E. Erdrich (Graywolf Press, 2018).

"The Second Gift" appeared in *Value of Hawaiʻi 2: Ancestral Roots, Oceanic Visions*, edited by Aiko Yamashiro and Noelani Goodyear-Kaʻōpua (University of Hawaiʻi Press, 2014), and in *Hawaiʻi Review* (Issue 79, January 2014).

"Hoʻi Hou i ka Iwi Kuamoʻo," "Star-Spangled Banner," "Postcards from Waikīkī," and "He Mele Aloha no ka Niu," appeared in *Black Renaissance/Renaissance Noire* (Volume 13, Issue 1, June 2013). "Hoʻi Hou i ka Iwi Kuamoʻo" also appeared in *MANA Magazine* (Volume 1, Issue 3, September/October 2012) and in *Smithsonian Magazine for the National Museum for the American Indian* (Winter 2009). "Postcards from Waikīkī" also appeared in *Capitalism Nature Socialism* (Volume 24, Issue 2, June 2013).

"Ka Hana Mau Loa" appeared in *Hoʻolauleʻa: Celebrating Ten Years of Pacific Writing* (Pacific Writers' Connection, 2012).

"Prepositions" appeared in *Ika: Journal of Creative Writing* (Issue 1, 2012).

"Poi-ku" appeared, under a slightly different title, in *Vice-Versa* (Issue 7, Spring 2011).

ABOUT THE AUTHOR

Brandy Nālani McDougall (Kanaka ʻŌiwi) is a poet, scholar, mother, and aloha ʻāina from Aʻapueo, Maui, and now lives with her ʻohana in Kalaepōhaku, Oʻahu. She is the director of the Mānoa Center for the Humanities and Civic Engagement and an associate professor of Indigenous studies in the University of Hawaiʻi at Mānoa's American Studies Department. Selected as the Hawaiʻi Poet Laureate for 2023–2025, she is the author of *Finding Meaning: Kaona and Contemporary Hawaiian Literature* and the collection of poetry *The Salt-Wind: Ka Makani Paʻakai*. This is her second book of poetry.